UNVEILED
AT LAST

UNVEILED AT LAST

BOB SJOGREN

YWAM Publishing
A Ministry of Youth With A Mission
P.O. Box 55787, Seattle, WA 98155

UNVEILED AT LAST

Published by YWAM Publishing, a ministry of
Youth With A Mission; P.O. Box 55787,
Seattle, WA 98155

All Scriptures are from the New International Version of
the Bible unless stated otherwise in the text.

ISBN 0-927545-37-3

Printed in the United States of America

Previously published under the title **DESTINATION 2000**

Dedication

This book is dedicated to the unreached Muslims, Buddhists, Hindus, Chinese, and tribal groups of the world. It is hoped that God will use this book to be a catalyst in sending laborers to start churches among the many unreached so that His fullest glory is reached.

A special thanks goes out to Don Richardson and Steve Hawthorne who have trained me in most of the material presented here and who continue to be my mentors in my pursuit of knowing the Scriptures.

Also, I wish to give special thanks to Bill Stearns, who so masterfully put the words together in this book; to Dorothy Schulte, who has labored faithfully at the computer; to my precious mother, who did the final editing of the first edition; and to Robert Hodge, who helped put together the second edition.

Foreword

For more than 40 years, I have been committed to helping fulfill the Great Commission. In fact, I try to evaluate everything I do each day in light of that
mandate—my speaking engagements, even the writing
of forewords to books, and writing a few books of my
own. There is no higher calling or greater privilege
known to man than being involved in helping fulfill the
Great Commission. That is the reason I am so excited
about *Unveiled at Last!*

This is a book which, in a way that is refreshing,
thoughtful, and thoroughly biblical, explores the theme
of the Great Commission and world evangelism as present throughout Scripture from Genesis to Revelation.
Bob Sjogren's study of evangelization in the Old Testament is particularly insightful. It is exciting to see such a
well-reasoned, motivating case for the unity of God's
Word as it relates in this instance to evangelization.

Bob Sjogren is in the midst of the battle, helping reach
the Muslim world through the dynamic ministry of
Frontiers. As he notes, there is still so much to be done
to reach the world for Christ, and the task before us
seems even more urgent as we approach a new millennium. *Unveiled at Last!* is an exciting study for any
Christian whose heart beats for the world!

Bill Bright

Contents

Introduction

Several years ago I was asked to speak at a conference in Mt. Pleasant, Michigan. The person who gave me directions from my home in Columbus, Ohio, said, "Just go north until you hit Detroit, take a left, and head toward East Lansing. There, you'll hit a loop. Start out at the bottom of that loop, go to the top, take a right, and that road will take you directly to our church!" Having been exposed to the intricate subways of Tokyo, I saw no problems with the directions as I looked at the map.

As my wife Debby and I were driving, we began playing the alphabet game to pass the time. Unfortunately, it was the wrong game for me to play because my wife "cheats." You see, her eyesight is better than mine, and she spots the signs about half a second earlier than I do. She's always ahead of me in the game.

Those who have played the game know that being ahead isn't a big deal, though, because once you hit the letter *Q*, everything stops. You're looking either for a Quaker State Motor Oil sign or a Quality Inn sign.

By the time we had passed Detroit and were on our way to East Lansing, Debby was on *Q* and I was on *B*! But it didn't matter. By the time we reached the bottom of that loop, we both were on *Q*.

Being the competitive person I am, I wanted to win, so I began squinting as hard as I could to see anything remotely resembling a Quaker State Motor Oil sign or a Quality Inn sign.

After quite a few signs, I finally saw one that said, "Detroit— 37." *Detroit,* I thought to myself, *that doesn't have a Q in it!* After a few moments it dawned on me.

"Wait a second," I said to Debby, "Detroit? Didn't we just pass Detroit about an hour and a half ago?"

Without realizing it, my wife and I were so focused on getting the *Q* that we totally lost our perspective of where we were. We had missed our turn, going totally around the loop and heading back to Detroit!

This incident parallels the way in which many Christians are living the Christian life. They're focused on the *C*'s of children's ministry and choir, the *D*'s of discipleship, the *E*'s of evangelism, the *F*'s of faith. These are all good things, but they're not the ultimate focus God intended. As a result, these ministries have become ends in themselves rather than means toward the end— God's "Big Picture" of redeeming people from every tongue, tribe, and nation.

This narrow focus causes us to err in two ways when reading the Scriptures: We view the Bible as 66 separate books and we insist upon writing ourselves in as main characters.

God is bigger than all cultures, and throughout history has revealed Himself as an absolute being who is able to be understood and known personally within differing cultural contexts.

Unfortunately, we only know God within the context of our one culture, and we miss out on the bigger, more accurate picture. With our mono-cultural view, we've limited ourselves to watching God on an old black and white TV with distorted sound and screen, and we've missed out on a multi-cultured, panoramic view of the God of the universe.

Today we must return to a deep study of the Word of God, seeking the role of our ministry in God's plan, plot, and purpose for the human race. To do this, we must be willing to end an affair with a Western society known for its self-centered, man-focused living.

We in the Church must view God as greater than ourselves and our culture, and learn to appreciate God's love for the diversity He has created. We must catch a fresh understanding that we are His creation, created for His glory. These will be accomplished when we, led by the Spirit, view God as the main character of His word. Then we will more clearly see that 66 books become one to present a divine purpose of redeeming people from every tongue, tribe, and nation, resulting in a greater glory to the Lord through His creation as we now know it.

1—Placing God Where He Belongs

Feel the wind blowing hot over the scrub in the foothills on the edge of the desert. Listen to the cracked, dry twitch of locusts. The sun is mercifully fading over this speck of southern Ethiopia. Night is coming quickly, prompting the lighting of torches in the boisterous encampment of the semi-nomadic Mursi tribe.

Sitting in the dirt next to Britisher Malcolm Hunter, you're a link in the great circle surrounding a festive stick-fighting ceremony. You can hardly hear Malcolm over the shouts of the fights and the lowing of the herd surrounding the camp. "Nomads are some of the most God-conscious peoples on earth," Malcolm says. "They live under God's stars, and appoint prayer leaders to pray to the Creator for rain."

Just then an entourage of seven warriors strides before you. They push a huge, muscled old man forward. Stoic as a statue, he's smeared with rancid butter and glistens in the firelight. One who can speak a little Swahili shouts to Malcolm, "He is your brother!" Malcolm looks at you. "I must not be understanding him. His Swahili is pretty rough."

"He is your brother," the warrior insists. "He has your blood in him." Through the evening, squinting against the swirling dirt of dust devils in the hot wind and listening over the cracks of the stick-fighting, you piece together bits of the story.

Saved by the Blood

Decades ago, the Mursi, now about 6,000 strong, were being decimated by a yellow fever epidemic. The tribe council finally chose eighteen of the strongest warriors to travel to the edge of the bush and find medicine.

After days of walking and near death from the fever, the eighteen staggered into a tiny hut that was a clinic staffed by a young American doctor. The doctor had himself been inoculated against yellow fever, but he had no yellow fever antidote. He didn't even have a way of taking blood samples from the dying men. But he did what he could. He inserted a needle into his own arm and began giving blood transfusions to the dying warriors, giving as much blood as he could without losing consciousness. Fifteen of the men died. Three miraculously survived. In fact, they were healed so quickly that they were able to head back out into the arid bush that same day. The last of those three legendary warriors stands before you.

Excited, Malcolm leaps to his feet and begins in pantomime and in "trade" Swahili to explain to the gathering crowd: "This mighty warrior is a picture to you from the God who sends rain. The God of the stars became a Man. He, too, gave His blood to save the Mursi!"

A World-Class Perspective

What is the significance of this true story? What is the purpose of including you in the scene? Try imagining God's perspective on what just happened. The God of the stars, of course, sees the big picture.

Look down on the nighttime Mursi celebration with its sudden excitement on hearing the white man's explanation of their tribal legend, of the significance of being saved by blood. Watch the tribesmen scurry over to the elders to pass the word. Notice how many of the people are limping, squinting with eye disease. Pull back and see the cattle herd grazing around the fire-lit encampment. Notice that the herd, the most valuable possession of the tribe, looks scrawny, sickly.

Glance across time. Catch the significance of God's grand orchestration of events over the years and miles with a mix of factors from yellow fever infection, to the young Dr. Barlow having no medicine, to a Malcolm Hunter studying nomads and happening upon this small tribe.

Now catch a vision of that grand orchestration. Come back in time and zoom up from Ethiopia to squint against the sun retreating across Africa. Peer across the Atlantic northward to the

Western Hemisphere, over the full daylight flooding the Eastern Seaboard of the United States to the flat wheat belts of North Dakota, where a veterinarian named Gerald is enjoying a lunch of bean soup and homemade bread at his kitchen table. Between bites he talks with his wife, a nurse, about a tribe he's heard of in Ethiopia. "I think they call 'em the Mursi," he says.

Look west across the Teton mountain range to the morning fog hovering over Washington State. Look down through the mist to see a small morning prayer group crying out to the Lord, responding to God's heart for the world.

Imagine the joy and sense of purpose that will strike the church members when God answers the longing of their hearts to be significant, to make a difference. Watch through the ensuing months as He leads them to invite a little-known missionary named Malcolm Hunter to speak, as he urges them to adopt a little Ethiopian tribe called the Mursi. Watch the spiritual fireworks when God convinces them to fully underwrite the support of a couple from North Dakota who are eager to go under the SIM International mission agency. Imagine the spiritual warfare all of these players encounter when the Enemy realizes one of his strongholds is threatened.

Today this drama still goes on. Veterinarian and nurse Gerald and Maija Carlson are, as you read this, living in a shipping crate on the back of a flatbed truck so they can be as mobile as the Mursi. The Washington church, Westminster Chapel of Bellevue, is praying like never before, sending short-term teams to Ethiopia and giving with a vengeance now that they're so clearly a part of God's big picture. They have made themselves accountable to God for the spiritual welfare of the Mursi.

Malcolm Hunter is pursuing his vision of waking the Church to its obligation to the 200 million nomads of the world who are, almost without exception, peoples without God and without hope.

But what about you? Where are you in this grand scheme?

Perhaps you're feeling restless to be a part of the thousands of daily dramas that make up the big picture of what God is doing in our world. Are you feeling left out of the heart of real, frontline Christianity with its blood, sweat, tears, and joy? Are you living a little life in a little world?

It's time to change all that. We'll study some verses, talk through some ideas, think together page after page, and we'll finally finish this book. But be forewarned: the time and effort you put into the book are a drop in the bucket compared to the flood of new insights, experiences, and big-picture involvement that will burst into your life after you breeze through this study—after you catch an age-old vision of your part in the history of the world.

Remember the Mursi. Pray for them as a people group to receive the Christ who gave His blood to save them. Pray for the Carlsons and others who are even now being prepared by the God of the universe for their frontline roles in His plan for southern Ethiopia. But pray as well for yourself, that you'll catch a world-class vision of God's heart, of God's perspective during this critical era of our planet. It's no coincidence that you're reading this book now, for you belong to a sovereign God.

The Protagonist

As high schoolers we were thrilled the moment our year-books finally arrived. Yet let's be honest—none of us looked for the principal's picture, and few searched out our best friend or sweetheart. We went for "good ol' number one." We wanted to see ourselves, and we studiously searched the index for all possible references to our names, eager to see our reputation rise in the eyes of the student body.

Little has changed. Over and again, as we "study" the Bible, we are really looking out for ourselves. Sure, we sing to God and talk a lot about Him, but even our songs ring out with words like: "...knowing well that as our hearts begin to worship, we'll be blessed because we came, O Lord, we'll be blessed because we came."

We talk about God and His power made manifest in our lives, but our stomachs soon draw our attention inward, and 30 minutes later we use our "battlefield communications system" (prayer) to call up a good parking space at a local restaurant. We love ourselves, and are really thankful that we can devote some of our time to a God who loves us even more.

Unfortunately, what we've really done is written ourselves in as the main characters—the protagonists of God's Word. Something's got to change, and we know what must be done. We need to die to ourselves and find out who the main character is.

If we confess Christ as Lord, His lordship must be increasingly evident in every aspect of our lives. Yet a death to self is only the first step in finding out who the true main character is of the Scriptures. It can be said that the Christian experiences four deaths in the process of maturing: death to self, death to family, death to country, and death to humanity.

All Christians are fairly clear about dying to self, and many strive to bring about that death to some degree. Some are aware of dying to family. Fewer die to their country, and very few understand the final death to humanity as a whole. And it is the final death—death to humanity—which enables an individual to see that the ultimate purpose of daily life is to bring glory to God.

Let's look at an example. Saddam Hussein invades Kuwait. American soldiers are sent over. What's the response of those Christians who haven't fully died yet? The self-centered Christian is more worried about the fact that gas prices are going up than anything else, because his pocket book is being inconvenienced.

The Christian who hasn't died to his family and friends is only praying for the safety of his relatives and friends who may be over there, or the relatives or friends of the people in his church. Not dying to your nation has you praying for all Americans that are over there and asking God to bring a quick victory so our soldiers can get back with fewest casualties.

With mankind as a whole as a protagonist, prayers are lifted up for justice to be done in that region of the world so that people can lead respectable, free lives. These are all good prayers heard by God, but they fall short. If you can see beyond what is happening to humans, you might see a bigger possibility of what is going on there.

God is acting on behalf of His own glory. Somehow He's moving in that region to bring more peoples to Himself so that their praise and glory would go to His name, from not only Americans, but also from Kuwaitis, Iraqis, Saudis, and Jordanians.

Yet few have died that last death and do not view the Bible (much less life) from a God-centered perspective. They are asking: "What can I get out of this?"; "What can my family and friends get out of this?"; "What can my nation get out of this?"; or "What do people get out of this?"

I've asked many audiences the following question: "Why did Jesus Christ come to the earth?" Ninety-nine times out of a hundred, the answer is the same. "To die for man's sin." A correct answer, but notice how man-centered that answer is. It revolves around what humans get out of it, not what God gets.

To fully understand the Scriptures, we must see God as the main character and ask ourselves the question, "What is God getting out of this?" Dying for man's sin wasn't Christ's ultimate purpose, for Jesus of Nazareth is quoted as saying that He came to glorify the Father, and that we in turn should follow His example and give our lives to the task of bringing glory to God.

Jesus Christ directed His attention to what God received out of His actions—glory—not primarily to what people got. It was Jesus who turned the attention of the woman at the well away from people and where they'd worship, and directed it toward God and what He was seeking—worshipers.

Worship goes beyond singing praise songs; it becomes a lifestyle continually pointing upward, honoring the God of the universe. Remember, He always has been, and still is, the main character.

Hence, each of us must ask ourselves the questions: "What does God get out my life as I surrender to Him? What did God get out of saving me? How can I please God by glorifying Him and directing my energies toward Him?"

Our understanding of God getting glory out of life heightens when it is brought into the context of diversity. Then the answer to the question, "What does God get out of world evangelization?" gives us the greatest purpose for life as we see God as the multi-cultured, panoramic God of the universe.

Ron is a friend of mine from Nashville, Tennessee. In the world's eyes, he's successful. He drives a nice car, has a beautiful home and a wonderful wife, and is good at what he does. He related an experience to me which resulted in his vision of God increasing dramatically. This story captures a principle which will help us see how God-directed praise can be maximized.

Having a heart for missions, Ron went to West Africa to visit a missionary friend. He started his journey by leaving home in his new car, driving to the airport, and eventually boarding a 747 toward his destination. Within hours he touched down in Africa, was met by his friend, and was driven out to the bush to meet some nationals who hungered to know more about God.

Within a relatively short period of time, Ron found himself praying not only with his missionary friend, but with a national believer who was quite different from him: he barely had shoes, his shirt and pants weren't decent enough for the Salvation Army, and he'd been walking for two days just to meet the missionary. As Ron prayed with his newly found brother in Christ, he realized that the great diversity between them had no negative impact on their unity in Christ. In fact, it made their unity much richer because of the diversity it encompassed.

This is when Ron's vision of God increased. He saw his Father able to transcend cultural barriers and even unify differences through Christ's atoning work. His glory to God was far greater as a result of the diversity that was now unified. Herein lies a powerful principle.

God gets greater glory as He, through Christ, brings unity from diversity.

In Revelation 5:9 we are told about a time when we shall stand before God's throne with people from every tongue, tribe, and nation. There, our vision of God will reach its highest point when we all worship God together in harmony! (Our knowledge of Him will as well, as we share our unique cultural understanding of our Father with each other!)

Anyone who has worked with internationals here in the States understands what happened to Ron. As they spend time with internationals, see them come to know the Lord from their differing backgrounds, and then pray with them in Christ's name, their vision of God increases—He gets greater glory from those involved.

With this principle, everything is in place to understand the Scriptures as a whole. God, the main character, is working toward the goal of attaining the greater good for all His creation. To give us a fuller understanding of His glory, He creates diversity (cultures) and unifies them (redemption) in Christ—for His sake and theirs!

This is the theme of the Scriptures—a unifying thematic backbone permeating God's Word from Genesis to Revelation. It allows us to read the Bible as one book, with one introduction, one story, and one conclusion with the main driving theme being God working toward the goal of bringing Himself a greater glory by creating diversity and bringing it back together in harmony!

With this God-centered focus, we are free to see our ministry as a means toward God's ultimate purpose, rather than an end in itself. Then we'll work with youth, not just to get them to say "no" to premarital sex, drugs, alcohol, etc., but to be holy and set apart so that they can later go out to the nations for His glory.

We'll work with adult children of alcoholic parents, not just to get them to learn to love themselves and others in an appropriate biblical manner, but to learn to live life the way God intended it to be lived so they can be free to share that love with others in their own culture as well as other cultures.

We'll trust God to heal marriages, not so couples can simply hold each other's hands and say, "Look what God's done in our marriage," but so that with a stable home, they can raise up godly children who will be ready to go to the world, and that their home could also be a second home to internationals from all over the world learning about the love of Christ in a family setting.

Seeing our ministry as more than an end in itself means we won't be caught "going back to Detroit." Rather, we'll be reaching His ultimate destination for our ministry, resulting in a greater glory from the nations.

For Further Thought

- Explain the four deaths which must occur before a Christian can fully understand the Scriptures.
- Think through areas of your life where you may not have died one of these deaths.
- Recall where you gave God greater glory, and see if there was diversity (problems, cultures, etc.) which was unified.
- Explain how your ministry is a means toward the overall goal of bringing God greater glory by reaching all nations.
- Begin looking for internationals whom God has put in your life, and seek to reach out to them.
- Pray for the Mursi of Ethiopia, who already are familiar with what it means to be saved by the blood.

2—God's Hidden Agenda

You're moving west around the globe, into the country of Mali in your trek across sub-Sahara Africa. With the Ethiopian Mursi people fresh in your mind, you meet up with a maverick named Randy....

Red, powder-soft dust billows in your window and up through the floorboards of the Land Rover. You're riding shotgun as Djibi drives and intently tells you a long story in a French dialect you don't understand. He watches your reactions for minutes at a time, smiling through the dust as you nervously worry about his staying on the track that wanders haphazardly through the West African 130-degree afternoon.

Lean Randy Cresswell, wearing hiking boots and sweating profusely, bounces in the open back of the Rover along with four more of his Muslim convert disciples he calls the "A-Team."

He tells you about last night's disastrous attempt to show the **Jesus** *evangelistic film in a tiny Mali village. Five minutes into the film, a wild wind storm leaped out of the desert to slap over the screen and knock the projector into the dirt. Now you're all heading to the village of Karaya. A Christian family hosting one of the region's first Christian weddings is planning to witness to their hundreds of Muslim relatives and wedding guests by showing the film. But the projector is permanently damaged although Randy and the A-Team stayed up most of the night trying to repair it. Jesus will be a no-show at the wedding, and you can tell Randy is feeling the discouragement of it all.*

You recall the passage of Randy's newsletter you'd read on the plane from Addis to Bamako: "The unremitting heat is balanced by incessant dust. Much more discomforting than this was a series of organizational decisions that were tearing me up inside. We just came out last week from under another financial crisis. The daily round of problem-solving seems to be grinding away what remains of my vigor and vitality...."

As you glance at Randy now in the back, he smiles back at you and tips his hat. You turn back to squint through the dirt-packed windshield, and wonder what drives a man to live on the edge of the world like this.

Cursed Traitors to Allah

Djibi pulls up under parched shade trees at the crumbly bank of the surging, half-mile-wide Senegal River. Randy climbs out, stretches, and says, "Must've opened a gate up at the dam. Can't drive it. Guess we'll have to swim."

Your voice creaks with dust: "Swim?"

He smiles, swings a blue nylon backpack over his shoulder, and scrambles down the bank. The A-Team graciously gestures for you to follow.

After the half mile of shoulder-deep wading, you emerge on the opposite bank in questionable shape for a wedding. The warm river water evaporates from your skin so quickly that you suddenly feel chilled.

Two young Kassonke boys from Karaya run to meet you. "No Jesus film," Randy apologizes, and they run back to the village a quarter mile away with the embarrassing, disappointing news.

In the village, so much preparation is going on around you that you're hardly noticed. That afternoon you trek four sweltering miles with Randy and Djibi to Djibi's village. When you arrive, his foster father stands in the doorway and refuses to allow any of you Christians, Djibi included, into his house. The man curses you as traitors to Allah.

You trudge back to Karaya to find a distinguished girot, a professional dance master, choreographing the antics of his dance troupe in traditional wedding dances. The parents of the groom dramatically apologize to each arriving guest, with a nod toward you and Randy, that there'll be no film as promised. There'll only be the dances. The usual.

"You okay?" you ask Randy, as you both, totally exhausted, lean against a rough stone corral to watch the dances.

"At the end of my energy, ideas, and emotions, frankly."

It's dark now, and the temperature cools to 110 degrees. Randy leans over to you with a glint in his eye. "Ask Toumani if he thinks I could portray the Crucifixion in a dance."

Toumani, one of the A-Team, says, "No."

Randy nods in the firelight and says, "I always follow my guys' advice. Almost always." But the glint in his eye remains.

Suddenly, during a lull in the professional troupe's repertoire, Randy leaps into the festivities, hiking boots, sweat-soaked shirt, and all, a crazy foreigner with a stick as his only prop.

The Messiah Dance

Something happens. The Kassonke crowds stop milling around the dance area. The faces are awe-struck as they watch this white man leap about, plod with a cross on his back, spin, hang on a crossbeam, die, and bury himself in the dirt. The air is electric, intense. The lone dancer stirs, then leaps into the air, alive again in resurrection. Dozens of Muslim men rush over to the A-Team with questions about the meaning of the dance.

After ten minutes of improvisation in a totally unfamiliar art form, Randy stops, beyond exhaustion. He, too, is besieged with questions. You understand some of the French: "What was the death for? He lives after the death? What does this mean?"

Randy staggers over to you and shrugs foolishly. He's painted in sweaty dust. The head girot rushes over and insists that Randy teach him this "Messiah Dance" and explain exactly what it means. The night crackles with the issue of the risen Christ as the disciples continue to field a deluge of questions.

After a half-hour's practice, the girot and Randy step together into the dance ring and, with precise movements, dance the story again. Afterward, around every torch, the entire village is buzzing with the story and the A-Team's explanations. By now it's about one o'clock in the morning. Randy motions for you to head with him down to the river to wash off some of the burial dirt. He can hardly walk.

Stumbling in the black darkness near the river, you suddenly stop and listen. The voice of the head girot grandly announces that everyone is to listen to the complete story of the Messiah

Dance. And you foreigners stand dumbfounded as the girot's voice rings out the explanation of the life, the death, and the resurrection of Jesus Christ. Some of the phrases he's borrowed from Randy's explanation; some from stories he's probably heard previously. But some of the truths this Muslim dance master preaches to the spellbound crowd are so biblically accurate and convicting that Randy shrugs and says, "Well, God spoke through a donkey, didn't He?"

The miraculous evening is only an initial breakthrough; no Muslims convert on the spot. But days later, as you head for the airport to fly out of Bamako to Casablanca and eventually New York, you hear that the Messiah Dance is being performed at wedding after wedding among the Kassonke people. At each dance troupe's performance, of course the Muslim girots must explain this new cultural fad's significance. Muslim dancers are proclaiming the Gospel!

At the airport, you glance at the note Randy handed you: "Paul says, 'The important thing is that in every way...Christ is preached. And because of this I rejoice' (Philippians 1:18). I firmly believe that God arranged the people and personalities, the weather patterns, and whatever else to bring that evening to pass, and I'm confident that He who has begun this good work, as strange as it is, will perform it until the day of Christ!"

You board the old prop plane to leave the dust and heat of Africa behind—the daily fare for Randy and other missionaries who are dead-set on reaching these unreached people with the blessing of redemption. You vow never to forget the crazy, striking scene of the first Messiah Dance. You pray now for the Kassonke to embrace that Messiah. Scratching your head, you are amazed at how committed God must be to this small tribe somewhere in the middle of nowhere.

Setting the Scene

In this book we are beginning to think differently about the priority of God's global purpose in the Bible. We'll see that the Bible, like any good book, has an introduction, a story, and a conclusion. The introduction is found in Genesis 1-11. The story starts in Genesis 12 and runs through to the book of Jude, while the conclusion is found in the book of Revelation. And on a touch-and-go sprint through the book, you'll see in a new way how that introduction, story line, and climax present the big picture of God's heart for the world.

Let's look at the introduction. God's first command to all mankind (Genesis 1:28) lays the foundation for God's eternal plan to bring Himself great glory. That plan was for humans to spread out and populate the planet. Such a spreading over centuries of time would have resulted in cultural diversities of language, food, clothing, and more. And as the creation would have maintained the practice of glorifying the Creator amidst the diversity, God would have been viewed as all the greater.

Yet God's perfect will was altered. Look at Genesis 11:1. This is where foul play inadvertently tries to derail God's will. "Now the whole world had one language and a common speech." What this simply means is that there was no "us-them" mentality. It wasn't "us" against "them." There was only "us." They were one people with one language and one culture. If their high school team wanted to play somebody in soccer, they had to play against themselves! There was no other "them" to play. The diversity God had planned had not yet come about. Being the evil mankind that they were, they wanted to maintain their oneness, make a name for themselves and conquer whatever other "them" there was. The only "them" was God Himself.

So the people began to build a tower that would reach to heaven. "They said, 'Come, let's make bricks and bake them thoroughly.' They used brick instead of stone, and tar for mortar. Then they said, 'Come, let us build ourselves a city, with a tower that reaches to the heavens, so that we may make a name for ourselves and not be scattered over the face of the whole earth'" (Genesis 11:3,4).

They wanted to make a name for themselves. Before whom? Again, before the only Other in existence—before God Himself. Bubbling up among them was tremendous pride as they determined to somehow gain equality with God! They knew that this equality could only be gained by preserving their outward identity as one people.

We all know that pride can destroy our relationship with God. God saw pride welling up to a point where He knew mankind would again, as before the flood, pass the point of ever again turning to Him. In order to prevent that, God made it known in no uncertain terms that they would not frustrate His purpose to have peoples. And if diversity could not come about through the natural process of diversity and cultural change, then He would make it come about supernaturally.

What should have taken hundreds (if not thousands) of years took place in one moment as cultural diversity was created by God at the tower of Babel. Instead of completely destroying the human race through a second judgment, God, out of His mercy, divided them up by confusing their speech, separating them into distinct groups of people according to language. It was a divide and conquer strategy. He divided them up so He could "conquer" (unify) them later with the Gospel, making this event an act of mercy more than an act of judgment.

If you count the number of groups listed in Genesis 10, you'll find that after the tower of Babel confusion of languages, there were approximately 70 groups of people on the face of the earth. God maintained His intention of being glorified through a diverse creation that was to return honor and praise to Him.

So at the end of the introduction to the story of the Bible, we have the major characters presented: God in heaven and 70 different groups of people on earth waiting to be unified in Christ for God's greater glory.

Now for the Rest of the Story....

Endure for a moment a loosely paraphrased Genesis 12:1-3 from the "Sjogren Revised Living Version." It goes like this:

> God looked down and saw 70 distinct groups of people, and He loved every one of them equally. He wanted to reach out to all of them with the blessing of redemption. He could have spoken the Gospel to each of them separately, but He chose not to. He chose to use mankind to

reach mankind, in order to prepare mankind in the process to rule and reign for eternity.

So, He picked out one man and said to him, "Abe, I want to bless you. In fact, I want to bless your socks off. I want to pour My grace upon you. I want to give you My word. I want to give you My Holy Spirit. I want to be your God, and I want you to be My people. The reason that I want to bless you, Abram, is that I love you, but also I want you to turn around and pass My blessings to all those 70 other groups of people that I formed at the tower of Babel, because I love them, too.

"Now Abe, you're not to just sit around in a nice easy chair saying, 'Oh, thank the Lord, I'm blessed.' You're to reach out to those other peoples and tell them what I'm telling you."

The New International Version goes on to say, "The Lord told Abram to leave his country and his people: 'Go to the land I will show you. I will make you into a great nation and I will bless you; I will make your name great, and you will be a blessing. I will bless those who bless you, and whoever curses you I will curse; and all peoples on earth will be blessed through you.'"

Abram (soon to be renamed Abraham) was to be blessed and to be a blessing to every people, tongue, tribe, to every distinct group of people bound by a common culture.

This message was given to Abraham in two simple parts, in what we'll call the "top line" and the "bottom line." The top line refers to God's blessing of Israel. He wants to bless His people. The bottom-line responsibility reveals that He wants His people to not only enjoy that blessing, but then to turn around and be a blessing to all families on the face of the earth, resulting in His greater glory.

Peoples' Power

The terms *families, peoples, tongues, tribes,* and *nations* are all synonyms for the same thing: groups of people that call "us" us and "them" them—people bound together by a common

language, culture, geography, religion, political system, etc.
Back in the time of Babel, people were only bound together
linguistically.

Survey your Bible concordance listings of the people-group
terms listed above. And remember not to equate peoples with our
idea of political countries; the Scriptures were not written in the
nineteenth and twentieth centuries. For example, the country of
India has about 3,000 distinct people groups within its borders,
Irian Jaya has about 250, the Commonwealth of Independent
States (formerly the Soviet Union) has more than 500 and
Pakistan has 13. Patrick Johnstone's book *Operation World* can
give more specifics relating to this.

The 70 people groups formed at the tower of Babel split into
about 60,000 by the time of Christ, when He commanded us to
make disciples of every nation or, literally, people group. Today
there are about 24,000 distinct people groups (a smaller number
due to communications, technology, air travel, politics, etc.).

Who are the unreached people groups of our planet? The
1,500 nomadic Chang-pa of Northern India, the 20 million
Sundanese of Indonesia, the Engenni of Nigeria, the Wenki of
China, the Gilyak of Russia, the Fulnio of Brazil...and about
11,994 more!

Twelve thousand people groups are currently being discipled. The other 12,000, mostly among the Muslim, Chinese,
Hindu, Buddhist, and tribal cultures, have no church among
them, and little to no mission work.

Look at that bottom-line message in Genesis 12:3; in one
very simple word. God said "all." All of the peoples of the earth
are to be blessed. That's a very significant word. God wanted to
reach every distinct group of people on the face of the earth. This
means what we actually have here in Genesis 12:1-3 is the Great
Commission!

Most believers think Jesus first gave the Great Commission.
Actually, Jesus reviewed the Great Commission. The Great
Commission was given to Abraham several thousand years ear-
lier in Genesis 12. Abraham was commissioned to reach all the

nations on the face of the earth, to "go therefore, and make disciples of all nations."

The Great Commission is the foundation for the story of the Bible. This commissioning begins a song that's sung from the very beginning to the very end of the story, a song we have in some of our modern hymnals: "Let every kindred, every tribe on this terrestrial ball, to Him all majesty ascribe and crown Him Lord of all...."

This story keeps going on....

God's destination for Israel was a land flowing with milk and honey. Does the Promised Land suggest the top line or the bottom line of blessing? The top line, of course. But with every top-line blessing comes a bottom-line responsibility. What is the bottom-line responsibility linked to the blessing of such a land?

The Promised Land was a strategic piece of property. It was located in the center of the nations on the face of the earth: "This is what the Sovereign Lord says: This is Jerusalem, which I have set in the center of the nations, with countries all around her" (Ezekiel 5:5).

Scholars say that most major trading routes of the world passed right through Jerusalem.

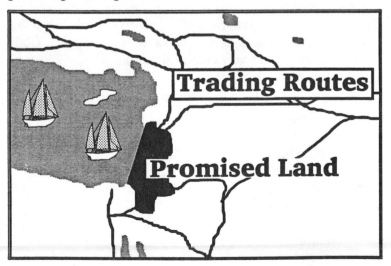

Imagine: While the merchants were trading, they talked with the Jews, asking them about their God: "Show me your god. It's going to be a rough trip home, and I need extra luck. So I'm offering sacrifices to as many gods as I can. Where's your god?"

And the Jews answered, "I'm sorry, we don't have an idol we worship. Our god is the God of the heavens and the earth."

They replied: "You're kidding! You don't have an idol? Every other nation does."

"We don't."

"Well, what's this god's name?" And the Jews began going over the names of God: Jehovah-Jireh, "God is our provider."

"You mean your god provides for you?" the traders asked.

"Yes, let me tell you how it happened." And they began testifying about how God provided.

"What? Your god is 'The Lord-Your-Righteousness'?"

"Yes," the Jews answered, "He is our righteousness."

"Tell me how you have righteousness through your god." On and on the questions must have flowed as people learned about the character of the one true God through His names.

As the caravans wound out of the Promised Land heading east, south, or north, this network of merchants kept talking about the nation that doesn't have a god they can see. The God of the Jews, they said, claims to be the God above all gods. We'll find later in our study that as this news began to spread, God's reputation went to the very ends of the earth.

Song of the Nations

Later in Israel's history, King David sings a prayer:

> Give thanks to the Lord, call on his name;
> make known among the nations what he has done.
> Declare his glory among the nations,
> his marvelous deeds among all peoples.
> Ascribe to the Lord, O families of nations,
> ascribe to the Lord glory and strength....
> Let the heavens rejoice, let the earth be glad;
> let them say among the nations, "The Lord reigns!"
> (I Chronicles 16:8,24,28,31).

Here it is again: the Great Commission, not in its original form but in a lyrical rendering of the Jews' bottom-line responsibility. It's a Davidic version of the good old gospel song "We've a Story to Tell to the Nations!"

Keep in mind that the Israelites sang these psalms regularly as one of the key methods of preserving the stories of their heritage from generation to generation. Poets and singers weren't incidental entertainers in most ancient cultures; they were revered as the historians, the keepers of tradition. For example, notice God's command to Moses to write down a song "and teach it to the Israelites and have them sing it, so that it may be a witness for me..." (Deuteronomy 31:19).

Let's go quickly on to Psalm 87 and see the story unfold even more. Most of us know there is going to be a book in heaven called the Book of Life. But did you know there is a whole library in heaven, not just a book? In Daniel 7:10 and Revelation 20:12 we have "books" being opened, in Daniel 10:21 we have the Book of Truth, in Malachi 3:16 we have the scroll of remembrances, and here we find another book.

The Register of the Peoples

Begin looking at Psalm 87:4: "I will record Rahab [Egypt] and Babylon among those who acknowledge me." Regardless of how we or early Israel viewed those groups, God states that the Egyptians and Babylonians were among those who acknowledged Him.

"Philistia too, and Tyre, along with Cush [Ethiopia]...will say, 'This one was born in Zion.'" Think it through: Were these Egyptians and Babylonians actually, physically born in Zion? Did they adhere to the dietary code or the customs of that time for the Jewish people?

If so, they would have been called Jews. But they're not. They're called Babylonians, Egyptians, and Ethiopians. They've been born into a spiritual Zion. Borrowing from New Testament terminology, we'd say they've been born into the Kingdom of God or the "Church." Now for a surprising insight into God's heart for every people group of the world: "'The Lord will write in the register of the peoples: 'This one was born in Zion'" (Psalm 87:6).

The register of the peoples! God has a book in heaven, and He's keeping track of every distinct ethnic group that has ever existed on the face of the earth—the bottom line!

God registers every distinct ethnic group that has ever existed because He made a promise to Abraham to reach every one of them, and He's going to be faithful in tracking that promise. He does not do it to jog His own memory, scratching His head, asking: "Hey, Abe. Did I reach those Kurds in Iraq yet? I'm not sure, could you check the register, please?" Rather, He's doing it to provide a witness and testimony to His faithfulness, showing that for all of eternity, He was faithful in blessing a few individuals from every people, tribe, and nation.

There are many references to God's global purpose in the Old Testament. We will catch more later, but for our initial overview, let's scan a couple of key New Testament passages. Does Jesus deal with the Abrahamic Covenant's bottom-line responsibility to be a blessing to every people? Or did He come to His disciples and say, "Look, you want to know why it's called the Old Testament? It's because it's old...outdated. Let me give you some fresh material, and we can call it the New Testament!"

The Upper-Room Seminar

In the context of Luke 24, Jesus had lived His life on the earth, had died, and had been resurrected from the dead after three days.

Notice that when He returned to His disciples, He wasn't telling them, "I'm alive again! Death has no hold on me. Let's praise the Lord together!" Instead, He was giving them the "Upper-Room Seminar," a forty-day crash course in reviewing the Great Commission. And that's where we find Him in verses 45-48.

"Then he [Jesus] opened their minds [the disciples] so they could understand the Scriptures." Catch the significance of this. Jesus was about to open up all of Scripture and explain it to His disciples. Don't you wish they had tape recorders back then!

How many themes do you think Jesus would have to address in order to do justice to all of the Scriptures? If I were to quiz you to name a major theme that Jesus would have to address, what would you say? Grace? Mercy? Love? And how many major themes would He cover? Ten? Thirty?

Interestingly, Luke tells us that Jesus broke down all the Scriptures into two central themes. Now let's be honest. If Jesus can take the entire Scriptures and break them down into two central themes, you and I need to be intimately acquainted with those themes, and should be teaching them to those around us.

Jesus says in verse 46, "This is what is written: The Christ will suffer and rise from the dead on the third day." That's the first theme: suffering, rising from the dead on the third day. He's speaking of the forgiveness of sins, about a relationship we can have with our God. And then He explains in verses 47 and 48 that "repentance and forgiveness of sins will be preached in his name to all nations, beginning at Jerusalem. You are witnesses of these things." The second theme is that His name should go to all the nations on the face of the earth.

Sounds a bit familiar, doesn't it?

That He should suffer and rise from the dead on the third day to provide salvation seems to refer to the top line. And that "repentance and forgiveness of sins should be preached in His name to all nations" refers, of course, to the bottom line of the covenant. We can thus say that Jesus broke all the Scriptures down into two central themes: top line and bottom line.

Now you have a concise answer for people who see you with your Bible and say, "Hey, what's the Bible really all about anyway?" You can tell them, "Two basic themes, since you've asked! God wants to bless you, and He wants you to turn around and be a blessing to all the peoples on the face of the earth."

Can this be true? Can you buy that? Let's put it to the test.

The Gospels tell of an expert on the Law who came to test Jesus. He asked Him, "Which is the greatest commandment in the Law?" What did Jesus say? "Love the Lord your God with all your heart...soul...and mind," referring to the top line. And, even though the questioner didn't ask for it, Jesus went on to say that the second is like the first: "Love your neighbor as yourself." This sounds vaguely related to the bottom line. But His answer doesn't have a specifically cross-cultural emphasis.

When the seeker asked, "But, Jesus, who is my neighbor?" what did Jesus bring in? The example of one from another people group, a Samaritan, a cross-cultural emphasis. Again, Jesus broke the Scriptures into two themes: top line and bottom line.

Look also at the Ten Commandments. The first four deal with your relationship to God—top-line stuff! The next six deal with your relationship to man—the bottom line of the covenant.

Is this new to you? No, not at all. You've just heard it in other phrases such as "to know Him and make Him known" or "your vertical relationship to God and your horizontal relationship to others." But now there's clarification. Our purpose is to make Him known to all nations, a horizontal relationship cross-cultur-ally. It's been there the whole time, but short of God's desire to reach all nations.

Obviously, if I'm focusing on the top line of the covenant only and saying, "I repent and receive the blessings of salvation, so God bless me, God bless us, God bless my family, God bless our church, God bless my community," I've missed half of Christianity. The other half of Christianity is turning around with that blessing and reaching out cross-culturally to the world.

Now, imagine that God had said to Abraham, "Look, I want to bless you so that you can be a blessing. Period." What would that mean? It would mean that all Abraham would have to do is reach out to people in his own culture, his own community, his own ethnic group, and God would be pleased. But God did not say "share this blessing with your family, with your neighbors, with people who are like you." He said, "Through you all peoples on earth shall be blessed."

God wanted Abraham to be involved in some type of cross-cultural ministry. And, emphasized again in the New Testament, He wants the same for us; He blessed us to be involved in reaching the nations. (We'll hit the implications of that mandate later, since most believers feel a little uncomfortable about it.) But let's plant it firmly somewhere in your gray matter: We believers are to have a cross-cultural impact in reaching all the nations to fulfill the promise God made to Abraham some 4,000 years ago.

We'll look more carefully through the New Testament later for this top-line/bottom-line theme. But for now, notice: When Jesus opened up the disciples' minds to understand the Scriptures, did He open their eyes to the New Testament only, to the New and Old Testament together, or just to the Old Testament? Of course it was just to the Old, because the New Testa-

ment had not been written yet. This proves that Jesus reviewed the Great Commission from the Old Testament, rather than giving it right before He ascended into the clouds!

Where do you think Jesus turned to in the Old Testament to prove that repentance and forgiveness of sins should be preached to "all nations"? Well, the text doesn't tell us, but we can make an educated guess that it was Genesis 12:3. How? Because now all of the disciples begin to quote Genesis 12:3, the original source Jesus must have highlighted in the Old Testament scrolls.

Later, Peter, standing before the Sanhedrin in Acts 3:25-26, quotes from the second half of Genesis 12:3. He didn't quote the first part of the verse, because he knew they knew that God wanted to bless them. But he knew they were unaware that God wanted them to be a blessing cross-culturally. Paul, writing to the Galatians (a Gentile people) also quotes Genesis 12:3 (Galatians 3:8). The writer to the Hebrews quotes Genesis 12:2 (Hebrews 6:13-17).

What are they doing? They're quoting the original source that Jesus gave in that Upper-Room Seminar. It was as if He took out a pink fluorescent highlighter and went over the verse again and again! That's why they remembered it and quoted it first.

Do you see that Jesus never *gave* the Great Commission? He *reviewed* the Great Commission of Genesis 12, and the disciples quoted that original mandate in their writings. Because Jesus turned to the Old Testament Scriptures to prove that the Gospel was to go out to all nations, missions had to be firmly embedded in the Old Testament....That's why it forms the story of the Bible.

In Galilee and Jerusalem and Judea?

Let's look at a final passage in our sprint through the story of the Bible. In Acts 2, we find Jesus already ascended into heaven, and see the disciples obeying Jesus' words: "...You will receive power when the Holy Spirit comes on you; and you will be my witnesses in Jerusalem, and in all Judea and Samaria, and to the ends of the earth" (Acts 1:8).

Jesus told the disciples to go back to Jerusalem. Why? Many evangelical Christians say, "Oh, I know what that means. If we're to go back to Jerusalem, we're supposed to go back to our own community. The disciples were going back to their own areas, their own towns. We're supposed to start in Jerusalem, our home town. That's where we start sharing our faith."

Wrong....I'm sorry, but the disciples were not from Jerusalem.

Look at Acts 2:6: "When they heard this sound, a crowd came together in bewilderment, because each one heard them speaking in his own language. Utterly amazed, they asked: 'Are not all these men who are speaking Galileans?'"

Now, how did they know the disciples were Galilean? Because the disciples all had strange accents; they didn't speak like the people in Jerusalem. They were in foreign territory.

Why had Jesus told them to go to a place which was not their home? Verse five has the key. "Now there were staying in Jerusalem God-fearing Jews from every nation under heaven." Our God is a strategic God. He gave the Jews the Promised Land so they could teach all the nations by being in the center.

It would appear He said to go to Jerusalem because He knew that in Jerusalem there were God-fearing Jews from every nation on the face of the earth, and He knew that they would be the impetus to start a worldwide movement that would spread to the very ends of the earth.

Why did God have the disciples speak in Gentile languages? Likely to emphasize that the Holy Spirit was not given to them merely for their own enrichment, pleasure, and edification, but to show that the Gospel was for all peoples to the very ends of the earth.

It was a missionary move, strategically planned by God so that all nations would have a chance to hear the Gospel. God planted the disciples not in their home towns but in the most strategic place to further His ironclad promise to bless all nations.

This is the story of the Bible in a nutshell. It starts in Genesis and silently yet powerfully runs through the Old Testament and flows into the New Testament. It's a cohesive theme, unifying all sixty-six books of the Bible to form one story: God's desire to see every nation reached through the message of redemption for His greater glory. It's there.

The Conclusion

But how does the story of the Bible end?

In Revelation 5:9 we find a song that's being sung by the elders and the living creatures, and if the elders and the living creatures are singing this song, we can be sure that it is very important. Such a key song will probably be sung over and over and over again, so if you haven't memorized the song yet, you ought to memorize it before you go to be with the Lord. Wouldn't you be embarrassed to have to say, "Excuse me, I never learned this song. Are there any handouts, please; would you mind focusing the overhead a little better on that cloud...?"

Listen to the song. Imagine the melody. Try to picture the setting: The elders and the living creatures are gathered around the throne singing, "You are worthy to take the scroll and to open its seals, because you were slain, and with your blood you purchased men for God from just about every tongue, tribe, people, and nation."

Obviously, that is not what the Word of God says. It actually says, "You are worthy...because...with your blood you purchased men for God from *every* tribe and language and people and nation. You have made them to be a kingdom and priests to serve our God, and they will reign on the earth" (Revelation 5:9, italics mine).

The plan God laid out in Genesis 12 to reach every distinct ethnic group on earth with His offer of redemption is finished. The story ends; He fulfills His promise to Abraham.

But perhaps there is a doubting Thomas up in heaven who starts yelling, "Stop the music; stop the singing; hold everything! How do we know this Lamb has redeemed people from every tongue and tribe and nation? How do we know He's worthy?"

What's Abraham going to do? Is he going to walk hastily over to Thomas and say, "Look, Tom, you blew it down there on Earth; don't blow it up here in heaven. Just keep quiet"? No. He's more likely to put his arm around Thomas and say, "Look, Tom, go down through the clouds twenty kilometers and take a left." (Okay, guys, it's going to be kilometers in heaven, not miles; let's get used to it.) "Then you'll hit a thunderstorm. Take a right at the thunderstorm and there you will find a library. Walk in past three aisles and on the left you'll find a book called The Register of the Peoples. Look under the listing of every distinct ethnic group that ever existed on the face of the earth and see if you do not find at least a few individuals who are represented here from each group.

"You can check, Thomas, but I guarantee you He's been

found worthy." The Register of the Peoples is a written testimony of what He has done.

Study Break

Worn out after our run through the Bible? Provoked by more questions than answers? Great! Then you're primed for a bit more intensive study of the big picture of God's purpose and your part in it.

But before you rush into our next chapter, think through the following section. And be accountable: Pray for the events God is now directing among one of the planet's people groups yet to be discipled. Pray for God's blessing on Randy and the Kossanke people.

For Further Thought

*   To reinforce the concept of top-line and bottom-line blessings, write out an explanation of this idea as if to a child.
*   Count your blessings! Then, in each category, list a possible bottom-line responsibility that matches each blessing.

	Top-line Blessings	**Bottom-line Responsibilities**
Spiritual:	_____	_____
Physical:	_____	_____
Relational:	_____	_____
Financial:	_____	_____

*   List other ideas new to you from this chapter's discussion.
*   List questions raised in this segment of study.
*   Scan the chapter, noting especially meaningful references. Mark these in your personal study Bible.
*   Memorize Revelation 5:9 and pray for those Ethiopian Mursi people who will be there!

3—Exploring the Agenda

On your way back home, you hear about an unparalleled opportunity—meet with Greg Livingstone, the founder of Frontiers (one of the fastest growing mission agencies to the Muslim world) in the heart of Albania.

Your heart skips a beat. You grab the phone and struggle in your high-school French to change your plans in order to meet up with him. Within two days, you're standing with Greg on the steps of the Cultural Palace across the street from the main mosque in Tirana, the capital city of what had been the most closed country in the world.

"This is an incredible opportunity," Greg says, smiling broadly. "Just a very short time ago, no one could even think of entering Albania, much less doing Christian work. Yet God is now working in such a way that all of that is changed."

The Frontiers team leader, Vince, joins you and adds more details. "Last night, we held an open-air meeting on the stone base where a statue of Stalin had stood. We had a couple hundred people there with very little notice...and boy were they hungry!"

"Having been in practically every Muslim country of the world," Greg interrupts, "it's difficult for me to fathom the openness of these people. There was only one disagreeable person in the entire crowd last night, and we could have stayed there long past midnight with the people who wanted to hear more. They're like curious children who have been banned from listening to any religious conversation for some 30 or 40 years."

"They're like clean chalkboards," Vince adds, "willing to be written upon, especially eager to listen to Americans."

"Tonight I'm going to have the privilege of speaking in the concert hall at the Cultural Palace," says Greg. "It is being given to us at no charge because they are so eager to listen to missionaries—they even call us that without any negative feelings!"

"This is not an isolated meeting," says Vince. "We are hoping to have this every week, but it may need to be held every month because there are so many inquirers that we can't follow up with them well enough."

Your mind explodes as you try to take all this in.

"Yesterday afternoon Vince and I were admiring one of the posters for last night's meeting and invited some of the men standing around the poster. Immediately we were into an open-air meeting where they were very curious and, in a friendly manner, talking about God."

Vince sits down on the top step and continues. "There is such a tremendous hunger for spiritual literature here. If you took out a box of New Testaments, you would be mobbed and hurt as Albanians rushed to get them. If we had the workers right now, we could put them to work out in the villages where nothing is happening and they would have a church on their hands immediately."

"It's incredible," says Greg. "In all of my 30 years, I have never seen the openness that Albania offers."

With a complete change of attitude, Greg turns to you and says with tremendous seriousness, "When you go back home, encourage people to pray like never before for Albania. We need reinforcements: long-term workers, teachers, disciplers, those who can learn the language and work toward seeing the Church become a reality. This may be Albania's moment in history for the Gospel...."

The Commitment

God's promise to reach all the nations through Abraham was repeated four more times after its initial declaration in Genesis 12:1-3: twice more to Abraham himself, once to Isaac, and once to Jacob. But He did something very peculiar in that third reinforcement.

God repeats the promise a third time in Genesis 22:15-18: "The angel of the Lord called to Abraham from heaven a second time and said, 'I swear by myself, declares the Lord, that because you have done this and have not withheld your son, your only son, I will surely bless you and make your descendants as numerous as the stars of the sky and as the sand on the seashore. Your descendants will take possession of the cities of their enemies, and through your offspring all nations on earth will be blessed...."'

Read back through that rendition of the covenant to notice the top line and bottom line of the blessing. Then think through that peculiar clause, "I swear by myself."

In Abraham's day, swearing was the equivalent of signing your name on the dotted line. Today we sign our name; back then they swore by something greater than themselves. They'd swear by God, or by heaven, or by the altar. But when God wants to impress on Abraham that He is signing on the dotted line, how can He swear by anything greater than Himself?

The only thing that He could do to assure Abraham of the seriousness of this promise was to swear by His own name. He said, "I swear by myself." Forgive another loose paraphrase, but it's as if God said, "If there's anything you can bet your bottom dollar on, it's that I'll bless you, Abraham, and that you'll be a blessing to all the nations of the earth. This is one thing you can count on: It will happen!" God comes to Isaac in Genesis 26:3-4 saying (my paraphrase), "What I told your father, the same thing holds true for you. I'll bless you to be a blessing to all the nations on the face of the earth." He comes to Jacob (again, my paraphrase): "Jacob, I spoke to your father, I spoke to your grandfather as well, and the same thing holds true for you. I'll bless you so you can be a blessing to all the families on the face of the earth" (Genesis 28:14).

God expresses this covenant five times in this opening development of the story of the Bible. He uses this repetition to focus attention on the promise itself, repeating to make it a high priority at the very beginning of His word.

He must have done this because He knows how many people can major on the minors and minor on the majors. So He tells us at the beginning of the Bible that this is extremely significant information; this is what we need to major on—reaching all nations on the face of the earth with His blessing of redemption.

Quickly glancing through Scripture, we can see how this top-line/bottom-line story unfolds.

God's Bottom-line Strategies

Notice, for instance, the creative imagery God used to remind the fledgling Hebrew nation of His covenant with Abraham, Isaac, and Jacob. As the children of Israel journeyed into the wilderness, "they came to Elim, where there were twelve springs and seventy palm trees, and they camped there near the water" (Exodus 15:27).

An oasis with 12 springs giving life to 70 palm trees. Do those numbers sound familiar? Twelve springs could easily represent the twelve tribes of Israel. Seventy palm trees could easily represent the 70 nations on the face of the earth of Genesis 11. And the object lesson is obvious: The twelve tribes of Israel were God's provision to give life to all the nations now scattered to the ends of the earth.

Blessed to Be a Blessing

Speaking of lyrical renditions of the Great Commission, let's follow the story of the Bible into the Psalms. In Psalm 67 we find again the basic structure of the covenant given to Abraham. The New American Standard Bible gives us this translation: "God be gracious to us and bless us, And cause His face to shine upon us." You've probably heard the first part of that verse many times. Is it top-line or bottom-line theology? It's top line, which may be why it is so familiar. Then, as we're learning to expect, comes the bottom line: "That Thy way may be known on the earth, Thy salvation among all nations."

Read through the rest of the Psalm:

> Let the peoples praise Thee, O God;
> Let all the peoples praise Thee.
> Let the nations be glad and sing for joy;
> For Thou wilt judge the peoples with uprightness,
> And guide the nations on the earth.
> Let the peoples praise Thee, O God;
> Let all the peoples praise Thee.

The earth has yielded its produce;
God, our God, blesses us....
That all the ends of the earth may fear Him.

Notice carefully the final verse: "God blesses us, that...."
Why? "That all the ends of the earth may fear Him."

God blesses us to be a blessing to the ends of the earth. If we try to hoard His blessing for ourselves, we're missing half of what God wants—for us to be a blessing cross-culturally. With every top-line blessing comes a bottom-line responsibility.

The Great Feast

In Isaiah 25:6-7, we catch a glimpse of who is going to be listed in that register of the peoples. Visualize the future with Isaiah: "On this mountain the Lord the Almighty will prepare a feast of rich food for all peoples, a banquet of aged wine—the best of meats and the finest of wines. On this mountain he will destroy the shroud that enfolds all peoples, the sheet that covers all nations; he will swallow up death forever. The Sovereign Lord will wipe away the tears from all faces; he will remove the disgrace of his people from all the earth. The Lord has spoken."

There's going to be a feast in heaven where God takes away the blindness of the nations and brings representatives from each of them into His kingdom.

Crashing the Party?

Let's think together through Matthew 8:5-12, the classic story of the faith of a Roman centurion. Keep in mind the context: the Jews had been overrun by the Romans. The centurion in this passage was a Gentile, whom the Jews commonly referred to as "dogs." God's chosen people knew that God blessed the Jewish people, but believed that He did not bless Gentiles.

When Jesus had entered Capernaum, a centurion came to Him, asking for help. "'Lord,' he said, 'my servant lies at home paralyzed and in terrible suffering.' Jesus said to him, 'I will go and heal him.'"

For Jesus to say that He would go to the house of a Gentile was very much against the cultural norm (even though some of the elders were encouraging him to do this). But Jesus showed

parity (beyond the elders' encouragement) for the Gentiles, so
Gentiles could have a part of God's blessing. "The centurion
replied, 'Lord, I do not deserve to have you come under my roof.
But just say the word, and my servant will be healed....'"

When Jesus heard this, He turned to those following Him and
said, "I have not found anyone in Israel with such great faith."
He's talking about a Gentile who has great faith. He didn't
exactly say this to get on the good side of the elders, you realize.
He said it to teach them something. It inflicted a wound, then He
began to rub salt in it.

Notice Matthew 8:11: "For I say to you that many will come
from the east and the west, and will take their places at the feast
with Abraham, Isaac and Jacob in the kingdom of heaven. But
the subjects of the kingdom will be thrown outside, into the
darkness, where there will be weeping and gnashing of teeth."

Now perhaps you've read these verses and thought, *Lord,
this sequence does not make sense. We were talking about the
great faith of this centurion and then suddenly You're talking
about some meal up in heaven—something entirely different!
Why?* Let's analyze the sequence.

The passage says many will come from the east and west,
and Luke adds the "north and south." (Thanks, Luke.) North and
south and east and west of where? Well, where they were—the
Promised Land. What's north, south, east, and west of the Promised Land? The nations, peoples, Gentiles—which is another
way of saying "all nations on the face of the earth."

Jesus is saying there will be representatives from every
distinct ethnic group taking their places at the feast with Abraham, Isaac, and Jacob. (We're reminded of the passage in Isaiah
25 we looked at; there'll be a multi-ethnic feast in heaven!)

A feast is a time to celebrate. In many Middle Eastern
cultures, a good feast sometimes lasts up to a week. You can have
a feast to celebrate a wedding, a birth, a religious holiday.
(Today's "feasts" would occur any time you have a good excuse
to have a party!) There's going to be a celebration in heaven with
Gentiles from all over, and at the head of the table are Abraham,

Isaac, and Jacob. But why them?

Did you ever wonder why God refers to Himself as the God of Abraham, Isaac, and Jacob? Did you ever study their lives?

Abraham's life was pretty good. As the father of our faith, there were a few times when he flagrantly lied to try to save himself. But let's rate him 70% good, 30% bad; we'll give him that much credit.

How about Isaac's life? He didn't do anything great; he didn't do anything that bad. There's a hint in the Scriptures that he could have conquered some people through war, but chose not to. A boring list of accomplishments for a patriarch, wouldn't you say?

Then we look at Jacob—"the mischievous one, the deceiver." Jacob's sons lie to him his entire life about his favorite son Joseph. He and his family face famine, and they go to the Gentile dogs of Egypt to beg for food. Now, why would God call Himself the God of Jacob?

Why not the God of Moses? The events he did for Moses were very impressive in the eyes of the world. Fifteen hundred years later the nations still remembered the Red Sea story.

But God calls Himself the God of Abraham, the God of Isaac, and the God of Jacob because Abraham, Isaac, and Jacob were the three men to whom He made a commitment to reach all the people groups on earth. When God refers to Himself as the God of Abraham, Isaac, and Jacob, it's as if He's saying, "You want to know My calling card? You want to know what I want to be known by? I'm the God who spoke to these three men to redeem and to bless every distinct ethnic group on the face of the earth. That's what I want to be known for."

Now let's return to the text in Matthew 8. In this text we see that there will be Gentiles from the north, south, east, and west coming to a feast to celebrate something, and at the head of the table will be Abraham, Isaac, and Jacob.

They'll be celebrating the fulfillment of the promise that God gave to those three men to reach every ethnic group. They'll be celebrating forever and ever, marveling in God's glory. And you and I will be there.

Notice the text says the representatives of these people groups will "take their places," not "crash the party." They will take their places at the feast with Abraham, Isaac, and Jacob—places reserved for them.

The Great Re-Commission

I think we've caught the idea now that Jesus did not give the Great Commission in Matthew 28:18-20; He simply reviewed it. But let's look at the Great Commission again to see if we can find something new.

"All authority in heaven and on earth has been given to me. Therefore go and make disciples of all nations, baptizing them in the name of the Father and of the Son and of the Holy Spirit, and teaching them to obey everything I have commanded you. And surely I will be with you always, to the very end of the age."

Unfortunately, our English language doesn't do justice to these verses. There are four verbs in this passage. The main action verb is not *go,* but *make disciples.* This is the main emphasis Jesus was giving.

"Make disciples" isn't a mandate to disciple individuals as was ordered in II Timothy 2:2. What follows "make disciples" is "all nations." How do you disciple a nation? Do you pull a nation into your living room and hold a Bible study? Of course not. So how do you do it?

Jesus gave us the answer in the latter part of the verse: "baptizing them...and teaching them." Baptizing gets individuals to identify with Christ, to stand up and say, "Yes, I am one of His disciples. I identify with Him." Teaching them to obey the Scriptures is the second part.

What do we have when we have a group of individuals identifying with Christ and being obedient to the Scriptures? A church. What Jesus is saying is, "Go to every distinct ethnic group [nation] on the face of the earth and start a church." We have an equal-opportunity God. He wants every group of people to have an equal opportunity to say "yes" or "no" to Him.

It is this meaning behind Matthew 28:18-20 which is prompting churches all over the nation to adopt a specific people group and seek to plant a sister church there. In fact, an entire network (Antioch Network) of churches is working to figure out how these sister churches can be established in these unreached people groups.

The leaders of Faith Evangelical Free Church in Tempe, Arizona are examples of those who have chosen to make the bottom line a priority in their church. Let's look at their story. As they began to grow as a young church, they wanted to keep themselves debt-free. When it came time to add to their building, they also wanted to keep missions a priority. They set out on a faith goal of $200,000: 50 percent going to the new building, 50 percent going to missions.

Every dollar which came in was split 50/50 so that no one project would have a higher priority than the other. Over time, the leaders began to pray about adopting an unreached people group and begin a church-planting effort there. Through prayer and research, an Islamic city in the Middle East was chosen.

The church elders then wrote down the names of those in the congregation they felt would be good candidates for going and working among these people. Over a period of time, 13 individuals were chosen. As the leaders approached those 13, they asked them to pray about the possibility of beginning this church-planting team. Eight of those thirteen said they would commit to going overseas to help start the sister church. Now those people are in a training process, preparing to make their lives count where there is no church or witness about Jesus Christ.

Though having outgrown the new facility the church had built years ago, this 600-member congregation still keeps the church-planting effort at the top of their priorities so that finances are regularly set aside to send this team out. They've clearly seen God's heart for all nations, and are keeping it a priority.

The Open Door Fellowship in Phoenix, Arizona has adopted a people group in the Middle East and already has a team there. Hope Chapel of Austin, Texas has adopted a people group in Asia and has a team there.

A major shift is quietly taking place. Churches are beginning to shy away from supporting individual missionaries who come knocking on their door on a monthly basis. The churches are thinking more strategically about getting people from within their own congregations to plant a sister church among an un- reached people group.

Think about it: Perhaps the reason many believers are reluc- tant to see their lives focused on God's great purpose as revealed in the Great Commission is because they know making a disciple of every person will never happen. After all, Christ Himself states that the gate is small, and the way is narrow that leads to life, and few are those who find it (Matthew 7:14).

If we secretly think the Great Commission is unrealistic, that it only expresses Jesus' desire to see "all creatures" become disciples, then of course it won't be a realistic part of our lives.

But mark it down for now: we're to make disciples of all *ethne,* of all people groups. And you just might get excited as later in our study we see how realistic that mandate is: how many ethnic groups have been "made disciples," how many ethnic groups haven't, how much more we have to do to actually fulfill the Great Commission that God first gave us back in Genesis 12.

Yes, I'm talking about us, you and me, our churches, living within sight of reaching every people group on the globe.

Let's look at one final passage in the conclusion to the story: "And this gospel of the kingdom will be preached in the whole world as a testimony to all nations, and then the end will come" (Matthew 24:14).

And then the end will come. What is the end? Fortunately, this isn't a study on the mysteries of the end times. There are plenty of volumes that wrangle about the timing of that particular phrase.

But the essence of the statement is clear: there is a direct link in the Bible between the end coming and God reaching all the nations on the face of the earth. Why is God concerned about reaching all the peoples on the face of the earth before the end?

First, because He made a promise to Abraham. And if God does not fulfill that promise, what can God be called for all of eternity? A liar. Can you imagine believers in heaven saying, "Not bad. All the groups but thirteen are represented. Hey, who's counting? God almost fulfilled His word." God will not be called a liar for all of eternity; it is impossible.

Second, if all nations weren't reached, He would not receive the greater glory we could give Him from what we know of on earth at this point.

Write it down as a fact: All nations will be reached, and then the end will come.

For Further Thought

For individual or group study:

- What difference does a top-line/bottom-line perspective make on our understanding of Scripture? Complete the sentences below from a top-line/bottom-line perspective:
  God calls Himself the God of Abraham, Isaac, and Jacob because....
  Jesus never really gave the Great Commission because....
  The basic unifying theme of all Scripture is....
  Although other passages command me to be a witness to everyone around me on the home front, Acts 1:8 isn't just a verse about reaching my own neighborhood because....
- List ideas new to you from this chapter's discussion.
- List questions raised in this segment of study.
- Write the U.S. Center for World Mission or contact Frontiers (1-800-GO2-THEM) and ask how you can get your church to adopt a people group.
- Scan the last two chapters, noting meaningful references. Mark these down in your Bible, and remember to pray for laborers to establish churches among the hungry people of Albania.

4—Impaired by the Top Line

You're back in the USA, with your mind still spinning from the report you got in Albania. Yet you still need to get to the washing machine to get the Sahara dust out of your clothes from your time with Randy. As you load in the detergent, you're wondering more than ever how God's people in America fit into the closing stages of God's plan to bless every people group on earth. You know the history of the amazing Student Volunteer Movement and the resulting surge in mission activity bursting from this continent a hundred years ago.

You're probably aware of the wave of new missionaries who went out following World War II. They left houses and lands to make Christ known among the nations in response to General Douglas MacArthur's plea for American missionaries to go to Japan. But that generation is now elderly, retiring from the front lines by the thousands.

What will be our destiny in God's plan to penetrate the remaining unreached people groups of the world with bottom-line blessings?

As the washing machine kicks in, you feel a little unsettled about American Christians' preoccupation with top-line blessings. You remember a church service you attended back in the winter of 1980 during the Iranian hostage crisis, when 52 Americans were held hostage by terrorists in Teheran:

You saw the bright Sunday sky outside the vaulted windows. You were seated in one of the largest fundamental congregations in the country. The morning service was smoothly orchestrated; you had relaxed in genuine meditative praise while enjoying a sweeping choral anthem in preparation for the biblical message. Glancing at the order of service in the bulletin, you saw that Greg

Livingstone was scheduled to give a "missions minute."

"Right," you thought. "This guy's really going to be able to say something significant in 60 seconds. The one-minute missionary."

The anthem ended and a square man who looked like a boxer stepped up to the podium. Without so much as an introduction, he asked, "How many of you are praying for the 52 American hostages held captive in Iran?"

You, of course, raised your hand. All present raised their hands. "Wow, that's terrific," he said. "There must be 4,000 people here."

"Now, let's be just as honest; Jesus is watching. How many of you," the boxer continued, "are praying for the 45 million Iranians held captive in Islam?"

One hand slowly went up. Two hands.

"What? Only two people?" he yelled. "What are you guys, Americans first and believers second?" The ensuing silence was not smoothly orchestrated. It was a powerful 60 seconds you will never forget. He closed by saying, "And I thought this was a Bible-believing church!" and then sat down!

The Quiet Corner

In the last chapter, we touched on an idea that might be unfamiliar, maybe even a little uncomfortable to you: God loves other people groups just as intensely as He does His chosen people. The Great Commission to reach out to those nations on God's heart is at least as old as Abraham.

How firmly entrenched is the Great Commission in the Old Testament? Let's face it: If the Great Commission is the solid theme of the Old Testament, if reaching all the nations has been God's priority since Genesis 12, then it needs to be the major theme—the driving force—in our lives if we are to give God the greater glory He should have.

If using His people to bless all the nations with the offer of redemption isn't really God's purpose for His Church on the earth, then the whole enterprise of missions should be kept quietly in the corner of the narthex. To many of us, reaching the peoples of the world is a sideline compartment of Christianity. It's a bulletin board with fuzzy photos of couples and large families surrounding a faded map of the world stuck here and there with blue and yellow pins. It's a once-a-year dutiful mission emphasis that leaves us feeling faintly guilty for how good we've got it. Missions mostly belongs to an obscure church committee whose main job is deciding how to allocate the funds that are routinely designated for reaching the world's ethnic groups— groups that aren't quite as important as we think we are.

The New Math

To see if the Great Commission is actually foundational in the Old Testament, we'll take a close look at the tower of Babel. God instituted and created every one of the languages formed at the tower of Babel, right? And if God created every one of those languages, we have to assume that God must have loved every one of those peoples equally, because He made them all, along with their languages.

Now wait a minute. How does that last statement strike you?

Does God love every people group equally? How you answer this question has tremendous implications as you consider the Great Commission in the Old Testament.

In Genesis 12, we found that the top line plus the bottom line equal His covenant. We could designate God's desire to bless Israel as A, the top line. God's desire to bless all the nations can be B, the bottom line. These equal His covenant, C, His promise to Abraham.

So, we could say A + B = C, a simple mathematrcal equation. Any mathematician can tell us that A and B can have three possible relationships. A can be greater than B, A can be less than B, or A can be equal to B.

If A is greater than B, the Abrahamic promise is basically God saying this: "Look, Abraham, I want to bless you. I want to be your God. I want you to be My people. I want to pour out My Spirit and My love and My grace upon you because I love you. I want to do this because you are My chosen people and I am so infatuated with you. And if by chance, Abraham, some of the blessing happens to spill out into all the Gentile groups, hey, that's no big deal. I can handle it. But right now, I want to bless you. My love for you is far greater than My love for all the nations."

That's "A is greater than B." There are some verses which seem to back up that formula. In Deuteronomy 7:6 we find that God says, "[I] have chosen you [Israel] out of all the peoples on the face of the earth to be...[my] treasured possession." If God chose Israel out of all the nations on the face of the earth, that would seem to indicate that A is greater than B. God's love for Israel would be greater than His love for all the nations. Do you agree?

Could A be less than B? Could God's love for the nations be far greater than His love for Israel? Well, frankly, no one ever assumes that. There's too much Scripture saying Israel is His treasured possession, the apple of His eye, etc.

So the only other possible option that we have is that A is equal to B. If that is true, then what God basically said to Abraham was this, "Look, Abraham, I want to bless you. I want to pour out My grace and My mercy upon you. I want to be your God. I want you to be My people, and just as important, Abraham, I want that blessing to go to all the nations. I want to reach every Gentile group because I love them equally." A equals B.

What will it be? A > B or A = B? Can you imagine Abraham scratching his head, wondering which one God meant?

Let's look at a passage of Scripture that will help shed some light on the question. "For I have chosen the Levite tribe out of all the tribes of Israel to stand and minister in the Lord's presence always" (Deuteronomy 18:5). God chose the Levite tribe to stand and minister in His name always.

There are twelve tribes. Notice the phrase "out of all the tribes." Did God love the Levite tribe more than He loved the other eleven? No. But He had a special purpose for the Levite tribe. Overlay that simple concept on our understanding of Deuteronomy 7:6: "For the Lord your God has chosen you out of all the peoples on the face of the earth to be his people, his treasured possession." Does this mean God has a special love for Israel at the exclusion of other peoples? Try this on for size: A = B. God has a special purpose for Israel and an equal love for all nations.

As we'll see, whether we look at the world through an A > B or through an A = B perspective makes a remarkable difference in what we see. For example, if you have an A > B perspective, what kind of a stance are you going to take politically in the Middle East? You'll take a staunchly pro-Israel stance. If you have an A = B perspective, what kind of a stance will you take politically? Justice for all nations equally.

Our understanding of Scripture takes a different twist as we'll see when we begin to read it with an A = B perspective. (We're finding that many theologians have somehow been trained with an A > B perspective and that much of the teaching we get comes from an A > B stance.)

How about you? What kind of teaching have you been getting in your Christian upbringing?

Fill in the blank. "Be still and...." That's right, "know that I am God." Most Christians know that pretty well. That's because it refers to what part of the covenant? Of course, the top line. But how about the next half of the verse; do you know what it is?

"I will be exalted among the nations. I will be exalted in the earth." As we should have expected, the bottom line.

Most Christians can easily quote the beginning of Psalm 46:10, but they have no idea what the rest of the verse is. Why? They have been brought up under an A > B Christianity...a Christianity that emphasizes how God has blessed us but leaves off the bottom-line responsibility "to be a blessing."

You will find it very interesting to think through many of the lessons you learned in Sunday school growing up as a child. Most of the lessons you learned were probably top-line lessons only, and you may have missed half of what the Bible says.

For example, think of Daniel in the lions' den. What lesson do we learn from Daniel in the lions' den? That's right: Trust in God, be faithful to Him, and He will take care of you. What part of the covenant does that refer to? The top line. God wants to bless you. But is there a bottom-line lesson to Daniel in the lions' den? Yes.

Look at what King Darius does: "Then King Darius wrote to all the peoples, nations and men of every language throughout the land: 'May you prosper greatly! I issue a decree that in every part of my kingdom people must fear and reverence the God of Daniel'" (Daniel 6:25,26). Here we have a Gentile king being used by the God of Israel to evangelize the Gentile world.

Think of it. You're a Gentile king who's been conquered by King Darius. You view him as the king of all kings, yet this king who conquered you is "Federal Expressing" you a letter telling you to worship and fear the God of Daniel and the Jews, a foreign people he's already conquered. What are you going to think? "Hey, that God of Israel must be pretty powerful. Isn't He the same God that they say brought about those plagues in Egypt and parted the Red Sea? And didn't He also...." Notice how committed God was in reaching out to all the peoples. "Then King Darius wrote to all the peoples, nations and men of every language...."

God can use your life to make an impact on internationals around you, who will in turn go and tell other internationals about your God. The bottom-line lesson of Daniel in the lions' den is there as surely as the top-line message; we just have to have our eyes trained to see it.

The story of David and Goliath is another good example. What lesson were we taught from David and Goliath? We wimps can take on giants. Right. Trust in God, and we can take down all those bad guys—the top-line lesson. Is there a bottom line? Yes.

"David said to the Philistine, 'You come against me with sword and spear and javelin, but I come against you in the name of the Lord Almighty, the God of the armies of Israel, whom you have defied. This day the Lord will hand you over to me, and I'll strike you down and cut off your head. Today I will give the carcasses of the Philistine army to the birds of the air and beasts of the earth, and the whole world will know that there is a God in Israel'" (I Samuel 17:45-46).

How is the whole world going to know? Through merchants who would be bumping into a bunch of Philistines running scared. "Why are they running scared?" they'd ask. "That small boy just beat our giant." And it would be confirmed as the Jews would sit them down over coffee and say, "Let me tell about our little boy David and how he defeated Goliath, over nine feet tall!"

Do you think they kept that secret to themselves? No! They passed it on from town to town, becoming human "traveling newspapers" spreading the news.

Who got the credit for that victory, David or the God of Israel? Yes, the God of Israel. With credit given to Him for that victory, it was His reputation that was scattered to the very ends of the earth. Those traders would pass that story along everywhere they went, broadening the reputation of the God of Israel.

The plagues tell us the same thing. If you have an A > B perspective, what is God doing with the ten plagues? He is lording it over the Egyptians, showing His strength, causing them to fear Him...with no hope of knowing Him.

If you have an A = B perspective, what is God doing? With this new perspective (and some study of Egyptian religion) you would realize that each one of the plagues dealt with one of the gods of Egypt. As each plague occurred, the Egyptians saw their gods knocked down. Of course they would begin to wonder, "Are we worshiping the true gods, or is the God of Israel greater?"

Did any of the Egyptians come to the conclusion that the God of Israel was greater? Look at Exodus 12:38. "Many other people went up with them, as well as large droves of livestock, both flocks and herds." Who were those "other people?" That's right—Egyptians. Remember God said in Psalm 87 that there would be Egyptians and Babylonians who acknowledged Him? God continually reached out to other peoples in the Old Testament through His miraculous work.

What about the Ten Commandments? Those were definitely top line, given to Israel to allow them to grow closer to Him and to walk in His holiness. Is there any bottom line in the Ten Commandments?

Look at Deuteronomy 4:6: "Observe them carefully, for this will show your wisdom and understanding to the nations, who will hear about all these decrees and say, 'Surely this great nation is a wise and understanding people.'"

When all the nations saw the great wisdom that there was in the Law, how were they going to respond? "Gee, great for them; sorry we can't apply it to ourselves." Or perhaps they would say, "Your God has given you great wisdom and insight into His marvelous laws. Can we know your God?"

Even the Ten Commandments were to give wisdom not only to the Israelites but to all the nations that would observe their laws. It was a testimony of the ways of the God of Israel.

Did you ever wonder why God gave Solomon such wisdom? Yes, He wanted to bless Solomon and His people. He is a God who loves Israel. But it doesn't stop with the top line. There is a bottom-line responsibility to the dispensing of His wisdom.

Look at II Chronicles 9:22-23: "King Solomon was greater in riches and wisdom than all the other kings of the earth. All the kings of the earth sought audience with Solomon to hear the wisdom God had put in his heart."

As all these kings came from all over the earth to attend one of Solomon's "International Wisdom Seminars," do you think they learned about the God of Israel? You bet. And do you think he told them the temple had a Gentile court? Yes, it was probably a vital part of Solomon's message to these kings.

God has blessed America tremendously with wisdom in our great universities so that as internationals come and study here, we can reach out to them in the name of Jesus—the bottom line.

Clearly, the Holy Spirit wanted us to see the bottom-line emphasis, for the inspired Word of God is full of top-line/bottom-line stories. Did you realize...

- Joseph was a blessing to the Egyptians (Genesis 41:14-49).
- Moses had a Midianite convert: his father-in-law (Exodus 18:1-12).

- Joshua and the spies were a blessing to Rahab of Jericho (Joshua 2:1-21).
- Naomi was a blessing to Ruth of Moab (Ruth 2:12).
- David reached out to the Gibeonites for the sake of the bottom line (II Samuel 21:1-14).
- Nathan rebuked David because he had put a Hittite to death (II Samuel 12:9,14).
- Solomon did some hard one-on-one evangelism to Queen Sheba (I Kings 10:1-9).
- The temple had an outer court dedicated to Gentiles (I Kings 8:41-43).
- Elijah blessed the widow of Zarephath (I Kings 17:7-24).
- Elisha healed the commander of the army of the King of Aram—Naaman (II Kings 5:1-26).
- Jeremiah was a prophet to the nations (Jeremiah 1:5).
- Daniel and his colleagues reached out to King Nebuchadnezzar, an act with international ramifications (Daniel 2:47-49; 3:28-29).
- Jonah reached out to an entire Gentile city—Nineveh (Jonah 3:3-10).
- God let the Ammonites know that He is Lord (Ezekiel 25:1-7); Moab, too (25:8-11); Edom as well (25:12-14); the Philistines also (25:15-17); the people of Tyre (26:1-6); Sidon (28:20-24), and the nations (38:23).

God has given much "copy" to the Gentiles. Genesis 1-11 is non-Jewish, as well as the entire book of Job (written before Genesis 12, according to our best understanding). That's 53 solid chapters right there.

Not only those, but the books of Ruth, Esther, Obadiah, Jonah, and Nahum show direct Gentile interaction. A third of the Psalms address the Gentiles positively! All of the Proverbs, Ecclesiastes, and the Song of Solomon were written in a generic sense as if to all mankind. Who knows, they may have been the handouts at Solomon's International Wisdom Seminars!

Luke, a Gentile, wrote 52 solid chapters of the New Testament. Four of the five women mentioned in the lineage of Jesus Christ were Gentiles. And most of the letters written in the New Testament were to Gentiles.

Of course we don't need to go on. You're getting the picture. Large amounts of Scripture have been dedicated to the Gentiles, the peoples that God loves as much as His beloved Jews.

Story after story in the Bible has both a top-line message and a bottom-line message. If you were brought up learning only top-line lessons, you may have missed half of what the Bible is trying to tell you. Don't be discouraged. With this new perspective, you are going to see the Scriptures come alive as you see God's heart in a whole new way.

Let's see practically how this preoccupation with the top line can mess up our thinking with respect to God's will for our lives.

The Great Misconception

It's said that the average American Evangelical can name about four verses directly related to God's global purpose. A Milwaukee missions committee, recently asked how many they could name, came up with two: Matthew 28:19 and Acts 1:8.

But the average evangelical Christian can give four. Maybe some can say eight as they focus on the top line of the covenant. That would be eight verses out of 8,000 in the New Testament. Many Christians think that God puts about one one-thousandth of a priority on His global purpose, on what we call missions. Thus giving missions one week out of fifty-two would be giving missions a much higher priority than it is due, if indeed only eight mission-minded verses existed.

An overemphasis on what God is doing to reach the ends of the earth is even more pronounced if you consider the whole Bible with its 32,000 verses: 24,000 in the Old Testament and 8,000 in the New. Eight out of 32,000 verses—that suggests an even a lower priority.

Such a warped view would suggest to some that Jesus must surely have come to the end of His three-year ministry and at the last moment put His hand to His head and said, "Listen, men, I forgot to tell you something! Boy, is this embarrassing. I'm about

to go to be with the Father....You also need to know that you're
supposed to go and reach the nations. I know you've got lots of
questions, but I've got to go back to the Father, so I'll send the
Holy Spirit to teach you all you're supposed to know about this."
And that was the Great Commission.

As a result, we Christians sometimes subconsciously think
that God gave us missions to inspire the ambitions of zealot
misfits. Perhaps God knew He would have some hyperactive
Christians who would have too much energy to burn, so He
planned for them to battle writhing pythons and strike out across
the wilds in pith helmets.

This would explain how some Christians can view life like
a bookshelf. You've got a big book called *Discipleship* over here,
one on music ministry, hefty volumes on marriage and family
relationships, and several others. Then over there, way at the end
of the shelf, is a skinny little brochure. The title: *Everything You
Always Wanted to Know About Missions.*

As a result, when they find out about someone heading in
that direction, they can so easily say, "Why go over there? We
have so many needs right here," or the killer, "Why throw your
life away? You've got so much talent that God can use here."
They conclude that if you are to be involved in missions, you've
got to be "holy" or "called," and if you're not either of those,
you're to be involved in "good ol' regular Christianity," which
unfortunately, is usually an A > B "Churchianity."

Top-line focused Christianity can really distort our percep-
tion of what is on God's heart. With such a distortion, *every
decision we make will be faulty until we see God's big picture for
this world and His glory.* There needs to be a clear understanding
of this thematic backbone of Scripture before we can best direct
our lives in this fast-paced world.

For Further Thought

- To reinforce the concept of people groups' equality before God, write out an explanation of $A + B = C$, $A > B$, and $A = B$, as if to a child.
- List other ideas new to you from this chapter's discussion.
- List questions raised in this segment of study.
- Scan the chapters, noting especially meaningful references and mark these in your Bible.
- Evaluate your life for any pronounced $A > B$ tendencies: Notice your prayer life, your calendar, your study of world news versus local or national news, your preparations for and dreams of the future.
- Pray that Christians in America will be Christians first and North Americans second.

5—Going Below the Surface

You remember having come back home from that church service a little shaken. Those sixty seconds were more powerful than the sermon itself. But is it still true today? Are we really North Americans first and Christians second?

Before you head out on your next trip, you need to spend some time with your little brother. He's missed you, and he's going to miss you more. So you nestle up beside him and begin to watch the "Sunday Sing-along," his favorite video tape. After three songs, a thought pops into your mind. "That's interesting. The last three songs dealt only with the top line of the covenant."

Reaching for the box, you begin to scan over the songs and think through the words. Of the 14 songs, only two of them deal with the bottom line...and you are being gracious in giving those two bottom-line credit!

Wow, is your little brother getting top-line Christianity only? You begin to wonder how much this infatuation with the top line of the covenant permeates our culture.

Later that day, with pen in hand, you turn your radio to a Christian station to listen to the songs. You are shocked! Ninety-five percent of the songs deal with the top line, "God wants to bless you." There is little emphasis on the bottom line

"Hey, let's push this further," you think. Getting in your '69 Volkswagen beetle, you head for the largest Christian bookstore in town. Walking in, you spot the manager, an old high school friend. You head over there, and, after some small talk, ask him what the majority of the books in his store deal with.

"That's an interesting question," he says. "Eighty-five percent of our books deal with how you can grow in your relationship with the Lord. We are really excited about that because we really

believe in ministering to the saints."

"Where is the missions section?" you ask.

"Oh, it's over there, that bottom row of books in the corner."
You walk in that direction and find that out of the 400-500 books
in the store, 14 deal with the bottom line. Are we so infatuated
with ourselves that we've missed half of what the Bible says?

The clincher comes when he excitedly hands you a brochure
on a conference that's coming up. "I hope you can be there. It's
going to be powerful!" As you hear his words trail away you
wonder what type of teaching these people are going to get. Top
speakers from around the nation will be addressing the theme
"To Run and Not Grow Weary." You check out the titles of the
keynote addresses—all top line. You then read through the list of
seminar electives and check for bottom-line titles: two out of 60.

Unfortunately, we're usually Americans first and Christians
second, and our teaching reflects it. Instead of looking out first
for God's kingdom, we are usually so concerned about ourselves
that we have missed the very heart of God.

Israel, a Great Commission Nation

Let's catch a fresh perspective on the Old Testament by
viewing it from the A = B perspective. Remember, God wanted
not only to bless Israel, but also to reach out to all the nations.
So it should be no surprise to discover that the Old Testament is
filled with references to the nations, the peoples, the Gentiles—
all the people groups on earth other than the Israelites.

Look back at Genesis 26:4 as the Abrahamic Covenant is
repeated to Isaac: "I will make your descendants as numerous as
the stars in the sky and will give them all these lands, and through
your offspring all nations on earth will be blessed."

When we think about the stars in the sky, we immediately
think of top-line lessons having to do with their number: Isaac
will have thousands, millions, billions of descendants. But this
imagery also has a secondary bottom-line meaning. Stars shine.
Isaac's descendants would be shining representatives of God to
whom? To all nations.

In tracing this recurring image through the Bible, we learn

God's people are to bring light to all people groups, all nations, all the Gentiles. Notice the obvious point of this metaphor in passages such as Simeon's prayer when the infant Jesus is presented in the temple: "My eyes have seen your salvation...a light for revelation to the Gentiles" (Luke 2:30-32). Jesus, born through the chosen people of Israel, is the Light of the Jews? Yes, but He's also the Light of the entire world.

Later, God repeats the covenant to Jacob with more imagery. He says, "Your descendants will be like the dust of the earth" (Genesis 28:14). Again, the image suggests the amazing number of Jacob's descendants. But there's more than just a top-line lesson.

If you've ever traveled in the Middle East, you know all about dust. Actually, if you've ever cleaned house, you know about dust; when it gets kicked up, it scatters all over. Jacob's descendants will be like the dust of the earth and "will spread out to the west and to the east, to the north and to the south." Do those phrases sound familiar?

Of course. We recognize them from Matthew 8, where Jesus says there will be people from the north, the south, the east and the west who take their places at the feast with Abraham, Isaac, and Jacob.

What is the result of their spreading out? Read the rest of Genesis 28:14: "All peoples on earth will be blessed through you and your offspring." All the nations will be "dusted" with God's blessing—the bottom line.

Dust doesn't form in a pile, nor do stars stay clumped together in one part of the sky.

Dusty Missionaries

God had a two-tiered strategy for world evangelization in the Old Testament. Remember His first strategy involved the central location of the Promised Land. The world's traders would come through Israel and take home the message of God's redemption. The nations would come to Israel, where His people would sparkle with the light of salvation.

The second tier of God's Old Testament strategy to evangelize the world involved sending Israel as a missionary nation. Israel would go and infiltrate like dust or sand into every nook and cranny of the nations of the earth, whether they wanted to or not. The Genesis 28 imagery suggests the Great Commission in another form: Go therefore, and make disciples of all nations. Spread out like the dust of the earth, and all nations north, south, east, and west of you will be blessed.

Why is Israel commissioned to bless other nations? Because A = B. The most primitive tribe in the remotest corner of the earth's wilderness was as important to God as His chosen people. God does not show favoritism between the Jews and any other people group on earth!

When we review old familiar stories of God's development of Israel as a nation with an A = B attitude, we'll find there are dozens of examples of God's missionary mandate to the Hebrews.

Try to rethink the familiar events of the Exodus with an A = B perspective. The central point of the record, of course, has to do with what happens within the Israelite camp. But the heart of God is intent on reaching all peoples. For instance, imagine what goes on in Midian as Moses leads the Hebrews out of Egypt.

"Now Jethro, the priest of Midian and father-in-law of Moses, heard of everything God had done for Moses and for his people Israel, and how the Lord had brought Israel out of Egypt" (Exodus 18:1). Is Jethro, the priest of the Midianites, Jew or Gentile? Gentile. From quite a distance, he had heard of everything the Lord had done for Israel. How? Was Moses faxing him? No. It was through the traders, those human "traveling newspapers," the most common way most of the world had of communicating. And what were they communicating?

Keep thinking through the context. There was no Old Testament world trade center that sent a memo out to all the eighteen-wheeler camels saying, "No one trade with Egypt. The God of the Hebrews is taking on the gods of the Egyptians, and it's unsafe. Once a victor arises, it will be safe to resume trading."

They did trade. Just think of the conversation around the

watering hole....

"Yeah, last time I got into Cairo, everything's covered with flies! So I ask, 'What are all these flies doing here?' And they say, 'Oh, well, that's the God of the Hebrews defeating the gods of the Egyptians.' Wild days down there. What kind of a god covers a country with flies?"

Another trader pulls his camel up to the well and says, "Wow! I wish I had a market for frogs. I could've really gotten them cheap there. You should have heard what they said all of those frogs were doing there...." At every watering hole, they passed this new information on. What was the world talking about? The true, powerful God, the God of Israel. City after city heard these stories through those traveling sources of information, and became impressed with the Lord.

As the entourage of Hebrews followed Moses to Mount Sinai, other events took place. God greatly protected His people. With an A > B perspective, you leave it at that. But with an A = B perspective, you're encouraged to view the old familiar story in a new light. Keep your imagination running for a few more minutes. With an A = B perspective, imagine the reaction of other people groups to God's leading Israel in their desert journey with the "pillar of cloud by day and the pillar of fire by night."

What happens in the desert during the daytime? It gets incredibly hot. At night it gets incredibly cold. Everyone watching this exodus of two and one half million people saw the pillar of cloud that came in the daytime. What did it do? It kept God's people cool. And the pillar of fire at night? It kept them warm.

Now, imagine you're a Hivite. You're in the Promised Land and you're looking to the horizon and you see a strange glow. You've seen it the past few evenings and you're curious. A trader comes by and you say, "Excuse me, sir, but could you tell me what that glow is on the horizon?"

He says, "Oh, that's the God of the Jews."

"The God of the Jews? They worship fire as a god?"

"No, He's a god that cannot be seen. He's the God of the heaven and the earth, they say, and they have many names for

Him." And the trader would list the names he had heard—God as Provider, God the All-Nourishing One, etc. He adds, "So their God is protecting His people in the desert."

You're really curious now. "He's protecting them in the desert?"

"Yes, He keeps them warm at nighttime with a huge pillar of fire, and He keeps them cool during the day with a cloud. You've seen those big clouds over there all day? That's Him, keeping them cooled off, protecting them during the day."

"Well, how do all of those people eat?" you ask.

"You're not going to believe it, but it's miraculous. I've seen it myself. Bread comes down out of heaven; they call it manna."

"Excuse me," you interrupt. "Is that the same God that sent all those plagues in Egypt that I heard about?"

"Yep, the same one."

"Is it the same one who brought them through the Red Sea on dry land?" you continue.

"Yep, same god."

"Wow!" Your mind races as you say, "Thank you very much, sir. I've been wondering for so long...it's kind of strange, though. It's been going around in circles for so long...." You turn and gaze at that glow over the horizon. Then you turn around and frown at a little piece of wood plated with gold, the thing your uncle made that you bow down to and you call your god. You say, "You know what, you haven't done much for me lately. In fact, you haven't done anything for me lately!"

And you look out again and watch the glow. You might easily say in your heart of hearts, "God, if I can know You, I want to know You."

Do you think the God of Israel would listen to that Hivite's prayer? Probably not, if A > B. But if A = B, that is exactly the prayer God would be listening for. God reached out to other nations by establishing a reputation for Himself through His chosen people.

Is the Task Achievable?

Is it obvious yet? God designated Israel to shine and spread the Great Commission news of God's blessing. Before we look at the obvious question of the Israelites' success at being Great Commissioners, let's look at another question: Was it practically possible for the children of Israel to accomplish this purpose?

In the beginning, giving a message to 69 other groups doesn't seem like too ridiculous a task for Abraham and his descendants. But some statisticians suggest that by the time of Christ, those 70 groups had splintered into approximately 60,000 distinct people groups!

It would seem impossible for the little nation of Israel, struggling simply to survive, to ever mount a realistic campaign of reaching other peoples with the message of God's blessing.

Perhaps you feel that way today about the Great Commission. It's a big world out there; there are more than five billion persons, with more coming all the time in alarming, exponential population growth. And most of that growth is precisely in the regions of the earth least penetrated by the Light of salvation.

For example, a people group you've probably never heard of is the Orizaba nation in the Mexican state of Veracruz. Think of 50,000 individuals, the direct modern descendants of the ancient Aztecs, with no knowledge of the blessings of redemption offered in Christ. Think of them dedicating their children to the spirits in hope of receiving blessing.

They're animists—spirit worshipers with beliefs that are perversions of Roman Catholicism. They speak Nahuatl, not Spanish. Mission groups' attempts to reach them with the Gospel have largely been met with disturbing accounts of spiritual attack.

Over the past 30 years, for example, a major mission agency has had missionary after missionary return from that field with a broken family, broken health, and disillusionment.

The Orizaba have been bound in the kingdom of darkness since before the Aztecs. And you're commanded to reach them.

Before you become too deeply discouraged, though, think through the astounding implications of a few lines from the beautiful song of Moses:

Remember the days of old;
Consider the generations long past.
Ask your father and he will tell you,
your elders, and they will explain to you.
When the Most High gave the nations their inheritance,
When he divided all mankind,
He set up boundaries for the peoples
according to the number
of the sons of Israel.
(Deuteronomy 32:7-8)

Interesting lyrics, aren't they? Why would God be diligent to set up the boundaries for all the nations in direct proportion to the numbers of the sons of Israel?

The proportion could be geographical limits to territorial domain. That is, as the people groups began to broaden and gain new territory on the face of the earth, God allowed Israel to grow larger geographically as well.

Or the proportion could be numerical boundary limits to population. Perhaps God determined the population growth of each people group according to the future population growth of the Hebrews. Perhaps He determined how many distinct people groups there would be on the earth in direct proportion to the number of the Jews.

Whether referring to geographical or to numerical factors, the meaning is clear: God had set the boundaries of the nations in direct proportion to the number of the sons of Israel.

And the point is this: If revival had ever broken out among the Jews, if they had caught the vision of reaching every people group for God, they would have been able to do it. Their commission was practical, possible. God's plan wouldn't allow the proportion of the number of His people per the number of unreached people groups to get out of hand.

The Great Commission, God determined, would be a realistic task that could be accomplished.

Go Ye

Was Israel really commanded to reach all the people groups

of the world? Yes. Even though we don't see the eager obedience of Abraham, Isaac, and Jacob's descendants actually going out to the Gentiles, we must not assume this is proof God did not want them to go. More likely we must conclude that this is evidence of their disobedience.

The Word clearly states, "Say among the nations, 'The Lord reigns'" (Psalm 96:10).

Did the Israelites ever realize how poor their performance was in obeying that command? Yes. The apostle Paul in New Testament times quotes Old Testament passages like Ezekiel 36:22 and writes that "God's name is blasphemed among the Gentiles because of you [who call yourselves Jews]" (Romans 2:24).

It seems that God's people should have clearly seen the seriousness of disobeying the Abrahamic Covenant's bottom-line responsibility. But, somehow, few of them felt the sting of their nation's dismal history of disobedience as acutely as the prophet Isaiah. Listen to his heartfelt lament:

> As a woman with child and about to give birth
> writhes and cries out in her pain,
> so were we in your presence, O Lord.
> We were with child, we writhed in pain,
> but we gave birth to wind.
> We have not brought salvation to the earth;
> we have not given birth to people of the world.
> (Isaiah 26:17-18)

Same Treatment

A does equal B; therefore, it makes sense then that God would treat other nations equally. For example:

We all know that the Jews were sent into 70 years of captivity. But did you know Egypt was sent into 40 years of captivity as well (Ezekiel 29:13)? Tyre was sent into 70 years of captivity (Isaiah 23:15).

God says the nations are just like Israel: "'Are not you Israelites the same to me as the Cushites?' declares the Lord. 'Did I not bring Israel up from Egypt, the Philistines from Caphtor and the Arameans from Kir?'" (Amos 9:7).

Why don't we have a record of all the direct dealings of God working with the other nations in Scripture? Because the world could not hold the books required to record it all!

So with its concentration on God's dealings with His selected people group, the Old Testament is, unfortunately, easily read with an A > B perspective. That's the stance even the prophet Jonah took as he ironically resented God's love for the repentant city of Nineveh (see Jonah 1-4).

What difference does A = B instead of A > B make in God's economy? Think of it this way: If A > B, then God's people can and should concentrate on their own welfare—their own growth and comfort—since they're more beloved to God than any other people on the globe.

Their prayers should rightly resound with pleas for more of God's blessing, with complaints about how unfairly they're being cared for as the world's prime-A people, with cries for Him to ease any of their suffering regardless of the suffering of others. It is of no great consequence if they don't get around to passing on bottom-line blessings, since no other group is really quite as deserving as they are of God's love.

On the other hand, if A = B, the entire picture changes.

Those "A people" who are blessed with top-line blessings are fortunate not because they're better than any other group; they're blessed first on account of God's sovereign, gracious selection. And since other groups equally deserve God's blessing, the "A's" are obligated to share God's blessings.

Debby is one of those "A people" who has discovered the bottom line in her Bible. Being a full-time mother, she realizes that she wants to pass on the blessings to other nations through her children. But God has her stateside raising a family as her husband works. As a result, she's been creative in implementing the bottom line into her daily life.

Now, instead of just teaching her children top-line verses to the songs they love, she's adding bottom-line verses. Her children are now singing:

The B-I-B-L-E
It has one story you see,
To reach all nations with God's love,
The B-I-B-L-E.

(See Appendix E for other creative bottom-line verses to familiar children's songs.)

It's this same emphasis on the bottom line which prompted a church in Phoenix to give their children the same vision for other nations. Using the book *From Arapesh to Zuni,* they had the children walk up in front of the church and hold up a picture of the people group. The children then told the congregation that this specific people group did not have the Bible in their language. After four people groups were spoken about, the children sang an old song with new words, substituting the name of the people group in each verse:

Jesus loves us, this is true,
But He loves the (Arapesh), too.
And this is His last command,
"Take My Gospel to each land."
Yes, Jesus loves them,
Yes, Jesus loves them,
Yes, Jesus loves them,
The Bible tells me so.

Miles away in a small prayer meeting on the campus of the U.S. Center for World Mission, a group of people had gathered to pray for a court decision which was going to challenge Roe v. Wade. During that prayer meeting, many prayers were lifted up for women thinking about getting abortions, and for the children who would potentially be aborted.

It was in that context that a bottom-line prayer got slipped in. "And Father, we pray that some of these women who choose not to murder their children will come to know You, and not only grow in that relationship, but would be so captivated by who You are that they would want to go out and stop abortions in Russia, where abortions are eight times what they are here in the United States" (Target Earth Data/Global Mapping; 1987 data).

Opportunities to apply the bottom line in our daily lives are everywhere. If you put on a piece of clothing made in another country, pray for that country. If you have to wait in line, choose a country and begin praying for laborers from your church to go to them. Families are giving up their vacation time to help agencies either overseas or at their home bases. Golden-Agers are retiring to the mission field rather than to condos on a golf course.

Implementing the bottom line is easy when you look for the opportunities. (For a listing of creative ways, see Appendix C.)

We must see that everything we do is merely a means toward the overall goal of what God is doing—redeeming people from every tongue, tribe, and nation for His greater glory. When we catch this perspective, we will fully understand that it is not our goals and dreams that count, but how our lives fit into what God is doing on a global scale.

Selah is a wonderful Hebrew term used often in the Psalms that suggests we pause and meditate on how a passage applies to our own lives. So read through those last couple of paragraphs, and *selah!*

Yet, getting back to Israel, what was God's reaction to Israel's poor performance record of following the Great Commission of Genesis 12? As we'll see in our next section of study, He mercifully sent them blindness!

For Further Thought

For individual or group study:

- Do some further study on how God used unusual missionary methods to spread the good news of His blessing of redemption:

  1. He allowed the slavery of a little girl to reach a Gentile in graphic example of A = B. (See II Kings 5:1-14.)

  2. He orchestrated events so that the Gentile king of Assyria commissioned Israeli priests to go as missionaries to Gentile settlers in Samaria! (See II Kings 17:24-28.)

- With an A = B perspective, review several of your favorite

Old Testament stories to consider how the nations might respond to God's dealings with Israel.

- Explain some of the new A = B perspective you've discovered in this chapter to a friend who may not know the bottom-line lessons.
- Go to Appendix D and look over a comparison of two churches (both theoretical) and their perspective toward missions. Place a check mark by which characteristic is most often seen in your church.
- Pray that the Chinese church would catch a vision for the 30 to 50 million Muslims in Northwest China who are virtually untouched by the Gospel.

6—God's Mercy Through Blindness

Somehow your clothes got cleaned just in time to stuff them back into a suitcase. You're traveling again, seeking a global perspective on God's orchestration of what many are calling the final era of the Great Commission.

Your 747 begins to descend over Bolivia.

Your flight from Miami to La Paz has been uneventful, so you've had plenty of time to review your notes:

- *Africa—50% Christian by AD 2000.*
- *Africa's unreached people groups—several hundred Muslim groups and thousands of small tribes. Progress good.*
- *North America—70 million Evangelicals.*
- *North America's unreached people groups—dozens of groups of American Indians within its borders.*

You jot a question to yourself as you descend: Is America obedient to the mandate? Are those totally untargeted Indian tribes indications of America's cross-eyed preoccupation with the top line? If so, how long till serious judgment? Or is it happening already?

You remember how often you heard Christianity denounced as decadent and meaningless in your journeys across Africa and Europe. Why? Because the only contact millions of people across the world have with what they think is Christianity from "Christian" America is "Dallas," Halloween III, and Madonna! You wonder what America has done to the name of God.

The "fasten your seat belts" announcement crackles over the jet's loudspeaker in Spanish and English.

You glance quickly at your notes on South America's role in God's ultimate purpose.

Brazilian Evangelicals attending church now outnumber Roman Catholics attending mass. Brazil is now sending more than 1,000 missionaries cross-culturally.

Moravian missionaries in Suriname are now bringing people to Christ with the expressed stipulation that they have a part in reaching unreached people groups, particularly Muslims. (Although this is not a scriptural requirement for salvation, it's a great tool to build world vision into converts.)

Across the continent, a whole new generation of believers supporting themselves as ministers, teachers, and laborers has emerged. Students serving as "inside advocates" help in their own people groups and are penetrating as never before into others' Christo-pagan and animistic cultures in courageous, no-holds-barred missions.

God's reputation across the continent?

You're landing, and you stuff away your notes, still worried about that last entry. Since the era of the Spanish Conquistadors, how has God's holy name fared among the peoples of South America?

You deplane and walk stiffly among the European and Indian faces into the disinfectant smell and the here-and-there blasts of air conditioning of the La Paz airport corridors. And you immediately find the answer to your question by glancing at a discarded newspaper as you wait in line for customs.

The headlines shout: "Murder, Suicide Among Evangelicals!" The article hits only the melodramatic points of the incident....

A rural congregation in the Beni area of Bolivia, a group that identified itself as "evangelical Christian," held four days of prayer, fasting, and dancing to purify their church. On the fourth day, the group began some sort of ritual to cast out demons. Here the news report gets fuzzy.

In the ensuing helter-skelter of frenzy, six people were either killed or committed suicide. Local and national authorities are now investigating, trying to find out from the surviving evangelical fanatics what actually took place.

The article reports an intense public reaction: newspapers, TV, marketplace flyers all blame the evangelical community. Especially intense is retaliation against foreign evangelical missionaries; most report threats of violence. Certain leaders of a national evangelical association were detained by Interpol, the international police. The Bolivian government used the occasion to reactivate an old law which requires all non-Roman Catholic religious groups to get permits for all meetings in churches and homes. They must register all members and submit detailed financial records to the government. "Evangelical believer" is suddenly a term associated with the People's Temple—Jim Jones massacre in Guyana in the '70s, another South American incident that soiled the name of God.

Waiting in line for your La Paz airport customs inspection, you feel nervous, conspicuous, as if you have "North American Evangelical" stamped across your passport. You're struck by how easily, with a little help from those who call themselves believers, the Enemy can blind the minds of the nations to the claims of Christ by tarnishing the reputation of the followers of the God of the universe.

God's Mercy Through Blindness

Did the Israelites know they were supposed to reach out to the nations? It's obvious through our in-depth study of Scripture that the Great Commission was solidly established in the Old Testament. The Israelites were obviously mandated to share God's blessing with every people group on the face of the globe.

Yet the apostle Paul, at first reading, seems to disagree with us, for Paul describes this idea of the Gentiles coming into the kingdom as a mystery, something not understood by the Jewish nation.

The Mystery

Paul writes in Ephesians 3:2-6: "Surely you have heard about the administration of God's grace that was given to me for you, That is, the mystery made known to me by revelation, as I have already written briefly. In reading this, then, you will be able to understand my insight into the mystery of Christ, which was not made known to men in other generations as it has now been revealed by the Spirit to God's holy apostles and prophets. This mystery is that through the gospel the Gentiles are heirs together with Israel, members together of one body, and sharers together in the promise in Christ Jesus."

Paul is saying that there's been a mystery hidden for generations, and that it's only now being understood. What is this mystery? This mystery is that the Gentiles are "heirs together with Israel."

Let's look further at what we thought was so obvious in even a cursory study of the Old Testament. In Romans 16:25-26, Paul closes his letter to the Romans with a prayer of praise: "Now to him who is able to establish you by my gospel and the proclamation of Jesus Christ, according to the revelation of the mystery hidden for long ages past, but now revealed and made known through the prophetic writings by the command of the eternal God, so that all nations might believe and obey him...."

There it is, the mystery hidden for long ages past, but now revealed.

In Colossians 1:25-26 Paul says, "I have become [the church's] servant by the commission God gave me to present to you the word of God in its fullness—the mystery that has been kept hidden for ages and generations, but is now disclosed to the saints. To them God has chosen to make known among the Gentiles the glorious riches of this mystery, which is Christ in you, the hope of glory."

Here we see Paul addressing two aspects of this multi-faceted mystery: (a) that the Gentiles can know salvation, and (b) that the Spirit of Christ can actually be in you—*you* being the Gentiles to whom he is writing!

Throughout the Old Testament there is a strong emphasis on the promise that God is with you. (Sometime when you're ready for an especially powerful Bible study, get a good exhaustive concordance and follow the references to "God is with you" in the Old Testament.) But when we come to the New Testament, we find a whole new understanding of God's relation to His people with the revelation that God is in you, not just with you. That's the second part of the mystery, and it's pretty familiar to us, perhaps because it relates firmly to a top-line blessing.

The first part of the mystery, that the Gentiles are heirs together with Israel, isn't quite such a familiar study to us and certainly seemed to be big news to Paul's Jewish audiences.

Paul flatly says that this has been a mystery hidden for ages, even though we clearly saw it in our study through the Old Testament! Something is wrong here in light of our new A = B understanding. Let's find out what it is.

Look back at Colossians 1:25. Notice the phrase "the word of God in its fullness." What is Paul referring to here, the New or the Old Testament? Clearly Paul is referring to the Old Testament's terminology and message. That means that what Paul is saying is that this mystery has been there all the time (in the Old Testament), but that many just haven't understood that message in its fullness.

With that phrase, "in its fullness," Paul is also saying that all of the teaching they have had up until this time from many of their rabbis has been incomplete. (Maybe it came from an A > B perspective?) And now Paul is going to give them something that will fill in the rest of the story (the A = B perspective).

In Ephesians 3:8-9 we read the following: "Although I am less than the least of all God's people, this grace was given me: to preach to the Gentiles the unsearchable riches of Christ, And to make plain to everyone the administration of this mystery, which for ages past was kept hidden in God...."

Notice that interesting phrase "which for ages past was kept hidden in God." And now consider a couple of questions. If God actually chooses to hide something, who can understand it? Can anybody? And why would God put something into a culture and not immediately reveal its meaning? Or, getting back to our Bible study, why would God put something in the Old Testament Scriptures yet not reveal it to all, or not allow people to see its truth revealed?

It's a good question, one that requires a little digging for a somewhat surprising answer. Let's begin, of course, by digging back into the Old Testament.

Foundations

In order to fully understand why God would put something in the Scriptures and not reveal its meaning, we need to lay two simple foundations.

The first is that God knows of our future disobedience, just as He knew in Deuteronomy 31 of Israel's future disobedience to His commandments:

> And the Lord said to Moses: "You are going to rest with your fathers, and these people will soon prostitute them-selves to the foreign gods of the land they are entering. They will forsake me and break the covenant I made with them. On that day I will become angry with them and forsake them; I will hide my face from them, and they will be destroyed. Many disasters and difficulties will come upon them..." (Deuteronomy 31:16-17).

A second foundation is found in the story of Moses' defense of Israel before God. Remember the context. Moses had gone up into the Glory of the Lord, which can be likened to a consuming fire. After two or three weeks, most Israelites thought he was dead.

They turned to Aaron and said, "Aaron, make us a god." They melted down their gold, and later, out popped a calf from the fire. At this point God directed this to the attention of Moses, telling of their impending judgment.

> Then the Lord said to Moses, "Go down, because your people, whom you brought up out of Egypt, have be-come corrupt. They have been quick to turn away from what I commanded them and have made themselves an idol cast in the shape of a calf. They have bowed down to it and sacrificed to it and have said, 'These are your gods, O Israel, who brought you up out of Egypt.'
>
> "I have seen these people," the Lord said to Moses, "and they are a stiff-necked people. Now leave me alone so

that my anger may burn against them and that I may destroy them. Then I will make you into a great nation." But Moses sought the favor of the Lord his God. "O Lord," he said, "why should your anger burn against your people, whom you brought out of Egypt with great power and a mighty hand?" (Exodus 32:7-11).

Next Moses spoke of the consequences, should God destroy Israel for its unfaithfulness to Him:

"Lord, why should your anger burn against your people, whom you brought out of Egypt with great power and a mighty hand? Why should the Egyptians say, 'It was with evil intent that he brought them out, to kill them in the mountains and to wipe them off the face of the earth'? Turn from your fierce anger; relent and do not bring disaster on your people. Remember your servants Abraham, Isaac and Israel, to whom you swore by your own self: 'I will make your descendants as numerous as the stars in the sky and I will give your descendants all this land I promised them, and it will be their inheritance forever'" (Exodus 32:11-13).

We then read "the Lord relented and did not bring on his people the disaster he had threatened" (Exodus 32:14).

Ultimate Courtroom Drama

What was happening here? To put it into today's terminology, Moses basically appointed himself defense attorney for two and a half million of his own people down there at the foot of the mountain. Now, as a defense attorney, he had a tremendous challenge facing him, because the prosecuting attorney happened to be the living God.

To complicate matters a thousand times, the Judge also happened to be the living God. Thus, if Moses could win this case in court, he should be acclaimed as the greatest lawyer of all time, and every lawyer should have to study this passage to see how he did it. This is high drama in the ultimate courtroom!

What did Moses do? Like any good attorney for the defense, he began listening to every word of the prosecuting attorney to find out whether there was some little foothold, some leverage, to break open his case.

Listening intently, he caught a few crucial words. What were those words? Look back at the passage to see if you notice what Moses did about God's statements.

Look at verse nine. God mentioned that He would make of Moses "a great nation." Sound familiar? It sounded familiar to Moses, too, as his mind poured over previous documents that might have a bearing on the case. "I will make you into a great nation" refers to what part of the covenant? The top line.

In effect, Moses said, "Surely, Lord, if you're interested in the top line of the covenant, You must be interested in the bottom line as well." Therefore, as the wise defense attorney, he began talking about the Egyptians. Now, let's think through that. Why would Moses begin to talk about the Egyptians in referring to the bottom line of the covenant?

Well, let's suppose that you're an Egyptian. You're in the pre-exile days. You've been enjoying a good, comfortable, secure life. You've got your family. Your kids are in a great Pharaonic school and come home with pyramids stuck on their foreheads because they were good children. You've got a nice job. Things are working out pretty well for you. You've got Hebrew slaves. The women come in and take care of your home and sing songs to your little ones about some legendary God of Abraham, Isaac, and Jacob. The men are baking bricks and adding an extra bedroom to your house.

All of a sudden, a man comes out of the desert stuttering. This character demands an audience with Pharaoh and says, "Let my people go!"

Well, you and your fellow Egyptians don't think much of him—he's not too impressive by your standards. He does a little miracle with power he says comes from the invisible, living, and true God of Israel. Your magicians do the same miracle, but his snake eats their snake. You get a little worried, but there's plenty about magic that you don't understand. Then as time goes on, another miracle happens. Your magicians match it. Another miracle. They match that. Just magic, right?

A fourth miracle, and you hear that the magicians are beginning to worry. A fifth miracle. A sixth miracle. Things your magicians can't even touch.

All of a sudden the Egyptian magicians are saying to the Pharaoh, "This has to be from the finger of God. We're not even coming close to matching what He can do."

Now, if you're a sincere seeker and really want to know truth, you must be thinking: *Am I worshiping the right gods? The highest, most powerful gods? Or is this God of Israel really the true God? And if He is, maybe I should go out into the desert with these Hebrews.*

Like any human, you don't want to waste your life on a lie; you want truth and reality. And if you're worshiping false gods or lesser gods, you're living out a lie. Maybe you ought to break down and follow the Israelites into the desert to meet this true God.

But you're still borderline. You're not sure. You've got all this comfort, all this security. Why throw it all away? So you're wrestling: *Do I or don't I?* Another miracle happens. And a final supernatural blow brings the impact of this amazing God into your living room: every firstborn son in Egypt is miraculously slain, including yours. Including the Pharaoh's son, and Pharaoh was supposed to be such a powerful god.

This God of the Hebrews has finally gotten your undivided attention; the streets echo with wails of grief and terror. This is a God to be reckoned with, to be seriously worshiped before He decides to show more of His power.

Then the next morning you wake up and the Hebrews are gone. They've gone out into the desert. Yet in the market you hear that Pharaoh is going out to get the Hebrew people back, and you think: *This is it. It's our god, the supreme Pharaoh against this invisible God of the Hebrews.* Now there's going to be some resolution in your mind about which gods or God to follow.

Soon the streets are clamoring with the news: The Pharaoh

is dead! The Hebrews passed through the sea on dry land! Miracle of miracles! Then the waters closed on Pharaoh and all his chariots!

In the craziness and the grief of these recent events, you're almost forced to think: *I'd better find out about this God of the Hebrews and start worshiping Him. Maybe I can catch a ship across the sea and still catch up with them. But I've got all this security, my position and lifestyle, everything that's kept me comfortable here at home. Should I go worship the God of Israel? Should I leave all this for what I now know is the truth?*

Unfortunately, it's a predicament many Christians find themselves in today. "Do I leave comfort and security and head out—figuratively or perhaps literally—into the unknown desert of lordship to follow after God?"

You, the Exodus-era Egyptian, wrestle with it. The turmoil is welling up inside you. Well, one morning you get out of bed and stagger past your firstborn son's empty bedroom. You're grief-stricken, miserable. You couldn't sleep as you wrestled with your conscience...*Should I go, should I stay...go...stay?* You grab your cup of Sanka. You step out into the sunlight and pick up the Cairo Daily News. You open it up and are struck with the headline: "God of Israel Destroys His 2-1/2 Million Followers!"

You have just now decided whether or not you'd like to follow the God of the Hebrews, and your answer is, of course, "No way!" If one's God blesses like that, who needs enemies?

And as the headlines spread across the trade routes to eventually reach all the other nations on the face of the earth, whose reputation (name, honor, glory, character) would be destroyed? God's. And if God's character is destroyed among men, would many of these people groups He is calling to Himself respond? Probably not. Therefore, He could not fulfill the bottom line of the covenant and He'd be called a liar for all eternity.

This was defense attorney Moses' argument in the ultimate courtroom drama.

"But Moses sought the favor of the Lord his God. 'O Lord,' he said, 'why should your anger burn against your people, whom you brought out of Egypt with great power and a mighty hand? Why should the Egyptians say, "It was with evil intent that he brought them out, to kill them...and to wipe them off the face of the earth"?'" (Exodus 32:11,12).

In other words: Lord, Your honor is going to be ruined; I know we're a worthless mob and deserve extinction, but how could the Egyptians trust You, if You wipe us out (not to mention that other nations won't be interested in following You either)? "Turn from your fierce anger; relent and do not bring disaster on your people. Remember your servants Abraham, Isaac and Israel" (Exodus 32:12).

What was Moses referring to? The Abrahamic Covenant, naturally. God's name cannot be profaned among the nations, not because God has a fragile ego, but because they'll turn away from Him, and this would thwart the fulfillment of the bottom line.

With the realization of how crucial it is to keep God's character in good standing to fulfill the bottom line of the covenant, let's look at Ezekiel 20:13-14. There, God reviews Israel's track record of following Him, making specific reference to the golden calf incident we just studied.

"Yet the people of Israel rebelled against me in the desert. They did not follow my decrees...So I said I would pour out my wrath on them and destroy them in the desert. But for the sake of my name, I did what would keep it from being profaned in the eyes of the nations in whose sight I had brought them out."

"But for the sake of my name...." Another way of saying that is "for the sake of my reputation and purpose." God wanted to protect His reputation in the sight of the nations who had seen Him bring Israel out. Why was He concerned about His reputation in the eyes of the nations? Because they were to be the fulfillment of the bottom line of the covenant.

In verse 23, however, God announces His corrective judgment of dispersing them among the nations and scattering them through the countries. In order to understand what He did on that occasion, we need to think a little bit about our accountability before God.

Remember the scriptural adage, "To whom much has been given, much is required" (Luke 12:48)? This is talking about being accountable before God for the spiritual revelation (insight) which He has already given us.

Guilt is solely a matter of what you do, or do not do, before God. True or false? You're right, it's a false statement. Guilt is not merely a matter of what you do, or do not do, before God, but what you do, or do not do, in light of what you know. Of the one to whom much has been given, much is required.

Let's develop a diagram to clarify this. We'll start out with an arrow representing man's disobedience. As man progresses from the left to the right in time, he's getting more and more disobedient.

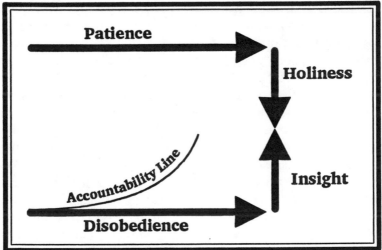

To the right of that arrow is another arrow ascending vertically. This represents man's insight into God's Word or God's ways.

Accountability is determined by the combination of what he does and what he knows. It could be a straight or curved line, or short and far to the right. It could rise up quickly and move very little to the right. It can fluctuate and go anywhere because it is a relationship of insight and obedience/disobedience.

Paralleling disobedience is another line representing God's

patience toward man's sin. As man's disobedience increases, God is patient. Yet even though unlimited in patience, He does act out of holiness, in His hatred of sin. That's the descending vertical line.

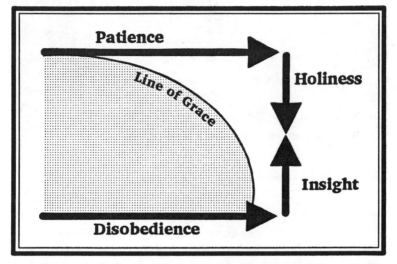

These two form another curve: God's "Line of Grace." On the inside of this curve, God's mercy is being patient with man's sin that is ever before Him. On the outside of this curve, God's justice prevails over man's sin.

It is possible for man's accountability line to cross over God's Line of Grace. At this point, God's call for justice is stronger than His desire to show mercy and the result is what we will call "judgment" (see graph on next page). It's as if God says at this point, "I will not put up with your sin any more. I'm patient, but out of My holiness and hatred of sin, I must act."

Think of some examples of judgment in the Old Testament. Sodom and Gomorrah, Korah's rebellion. In the New Testament: Ananias' and Sapphira's lie.

Try plotting those examples on your own graph. Plot the extremely low insight but tremendously high level of disobedience of Sodom and Gomorrah. God's judgment finally struck after a long period of disobedience.

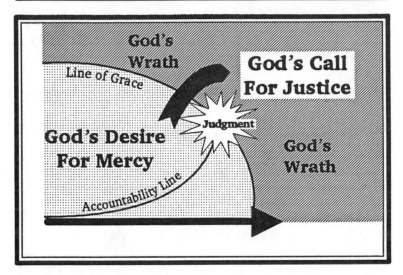

If you plotted a nearly vertical line that intersected quickly with God's Line of Grace, could it represent God's judgment of Moses? His insight was tremendous, and his disobedience in striking a rock seems minimal. But still, God's action in judgment strikes, and Moses pays the consequences of a little disobedience against tremendous insight by not being allowed to enter the Promised Land.

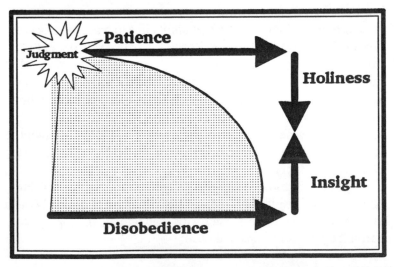

Notice that this judgment is not necessarily a question of going to heaven or to hell. Judgment is more often a practical consequence, a "reaping of destruction" (see Galatians 6:7), including physical death—being taken out of the game called life prematurely.

To sum up the point of this theoretical chart: There comes a point when man's accountability can cross God's Line of Grace, and then comes a judgment, when God will act out of His hatred of sin, in keeping with His divine purpose.

In Ezekiel 20:13 we read: "...I said I would pour out my wrath on them and destroy them in the desert." What does that sound like? Israel's guilt line was soon going to cross God's Line of Grace, and He was going to bring about a judgment. But if God did judge, what would happen? He'd ruin His reputation and never be able to fulfill the bottom line of the covenant among the Egyptians or any other people group watching His dealings with His people.

Therefore He says, "But for the sake of my name I did what would keep it from being profaned in the eyes of the nations in whose sight I had brought them out." What was the *what* that God did? What did He do to keep from wiping them out and ruining His reputation?

Think carefully and consider the following. God kept their accountability line from crossing His Line of Grace. His Line of Grace is consistent, but man's accountability/guilt line can vary. The guilt line, as drawn here, is made up of two components: insight and disobedience.

The "easiest" component for God to manipulate would be insight, which is what God reveals, rather than disobedience, which is based on man's decisions.

So let's propose that God brought over His people a cloud of blindness, a spiritual blindness, so that they did not understand the Scriptures or their prophets fully. And in not understanding them fully, they were less accountable in their disobedience. Remember, just as of the one to whom much has been given, much is required, the converse may also hold true, that of the one to whom less has been given, less is required.

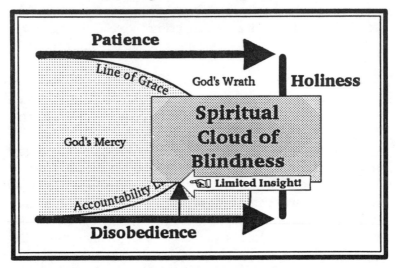

With this theory, we can say that as Israel's accountability curve was rising and would soon intersect with God's Line of Grace in judgment, God blinded their insight. He blinded them from understanding part of the Scriptures to keep them less accountable, so as to not bring about judgment, and to be able to attract people from other nations to Him and fulfill the bottom line of the covenant.

Now, to what part of the Scriptures do you think God made them blind? He blinded them from understanding their responsibility to reach out to all the nations. This would explain why the apostle Paul says it has been a mystery that has been kept hidden for ages but is only now being revealed. Why did He hide it? To keep them less accountable so He wouldn't have to judge them in the sight of all the nations. Because if He had done that, He would have ruined His reputation and not been able to fulfill the bottom line of the covenant. He did this because He knew of their future disobedience.

Why would God reveal it to the apostle Paul, and to us now, but not to them? What do we have that they didn't? We have the Holy Spirit, who gives us power to be obedient to the Great

Commission (Acts 1:8)—to keep us on the left side of the graph.

And so God in His great mercy blinded them to many aspects of His word, as He still does today! "But [the Israelites'] minds were made dull, for to this day the same veil remains when the old covenant is read. It has not been removed, because only in Christ is it taken away. Even to this day when Moses is read, a veil covers their hearts" (II Corinthians 3:14-15).

God knows our future obedience; yes, yours, too. He's giving us insight into understanding the true, big picture of the Great Commission. If He knows that our future disobedience is there, He'll blind us from understanding the Great Commission and we'll be less responsible for it, so that He won't have to judge us here on this earth in light of our insight.

Though God mercifully withholds further insight from us (which I call the "blindness option") we must each recognize our accountability before God for the insight we have already received. When it is obvious that we are being disobedient, our insight will not increase. Our disobedience is the barrier to further insight.

You say, "Yes, it's a great graph, but prove it biblically."

Hold on, and we'll see how Scripture backs this up. But for now, _selah_.

One short warning. This graph is not perfect. Don't try to pick it apart, apply it in every situation, etc. See it as a simplified explanation attempting to explain God's dealing with Israel in their relationship to the Great Commission.

For Further Thought

For individual or group study:

- Think through another exercise on looking at world events as God does. Quickly list two or three current events that have fostered negative reports about Christians or simply about "Christian" America. Then imagine yourself as a member of an unreached people group. How does that news affect your image of the true God?

- How could God use even those events to reach these

people groups with the truth about Himself?

- List ideas new to you from this chapter's discussion.
- List questions raised in this segment of study.
- List individuals from other cultures who may be getting their understanding of Christianity through your life.
- Find passages of judgment in the Scriptures and see where there was disobedience in the context.
- Explain the blindness graph as if to a child.
- Reference the phrase "I will hide my face" and see if there is any connection between this and blindness.
- Pray for God's reputation in South America.

7—Obey and See

You flew west out of Lima on a numbing 17-hour flight to Jakarta. Then you met the squirrely little prop plane which took you to Irian Jaya. And now you're in a Missionary Aviation Fellowship helicopter clattering over one of the most treacherous tropical rain forests on earth.

The island used to be called New Guinea; now this western half is known as Irian Jaya, one of the territories belonging to Islamic-dominated, animistic Indonesia.

Mike Meeuwse, the pilot, is singing, "I once was blind, but now I see...." He looks like Tom Selleck.

"So, tell me the story of this Nipsan tribe," you prompt.

Mike constantly peers around at the gray-blue thunderheads to the north and south as you approach a bank of cliffs rising out of the lowland jungle. The chopper cab is sticky and humid under the relentless sun. "Some of the most unpredictable weather in the world is right around here," he muses. He points to several thousand-foot waterfalls cascading from the cliffs as the helicopter banks into a canyon, heading for the primitive highland village of Nipsan. The site of a grisly massacre of believers fifteen years ago, today it is the site of a remarkable feast of celebration.

"There's a whole cluster of villages in the tribe. We just call the whole group after the main village, Nipsan. Garrett Khyte is the Netherlands Reformed Congregation missionary who felt led to reach that unreached group back in the early '70s. Like many of the other 250 or so people groups in Irian, the Nipsan were head-hunting cannibals. Not exactly the kind of place to raise your kids. But that's what Garrett did. Went in with his wife and family and started a school with the blessing of the Indonesian government. The Nipsan spoke a Yali dialect, so Garrett invited several Pass Valley evangelists who spoke a similar Yali to come as teachers and helpers.

"Then it started," his voice became more serious.

"Some of the young men at the school started acting like big shots around the village chiefs. And then the Nipsan chiefs started noticing how the Pass Valley evangelists and their families cooked their pigs. Seems in Nipsan, you've got to whisper something in the pig's ear before you kill it. The Pass Valley Christians didn't whisper anything; and they singed the hair off before they cooked the pig. So the chiefs became convinced that the Christians were releasing evil pig spirits into the villages."

Mike pauses as the helicopter swings between ridges, following a rushing brown river up into the highlands under the tropical blaze of the sun.

"Once when Garrett and his family had been flown out, the head chief ordered each village to invite one of the Pass Valley missionaries for dinner. As they arrived, the villagers attacked the wives and children back at the main camp. Fourteen men, women, and babies were killed and eaten. For the sake of the Gospel."

You bank over a light ridge and see a cleared valley with hundreds of scurrying figures, blurred by wafting smoke. You're suddenly concerned about this feast you've been invited to.

"A few believers escaped. And the head Pass Valley missionary, fellow named Saboonwarek, happened to be out of the valley. They got word to Garrett, so he had some of our MAF planes fly over regularly just to keep contact. The villages immediately had a catastrophic earthquake that altered the streams and completely ruined all their gardens. Reports came out of neighboring tribes that the Nipsan people were starving. So Garrett started dropping sweet potatoes out of the planes. But each time when they'd fly over the next day, he'd see the sweet potatoes chopped up and thrown in the river. That's how hateful and fearful the Nipsan were."

Mike begins the procedure for landing in the clearing as you peer down and see, for the first time, the stone-age Nipsan people group.

"One day, about four years after the massacre, Garrett told

the pilot to land. Then, this gutsy missionary steps out with an ax. A crowd of the Nipsan cannibals come rushing up. Garrett offers one of the men the ax as a gift. The guy slowly reaches out and takes it. Can you imagine?"

"And then?" you ask, as the chopper settles on the ground, swishing dust and the smoke from the feast fires in all directions.

"Garrett nods. The man with the ax smiles...which means they'll accept him again. So Garrett moves his family back in, takes Saboonwarek with him as the main missionary, and for the next dozen years sees the wildest harvest imaginable. Hundreds of Nipsan turned to Christ in wave after wave of conversion...an entire people movement to Christ." Mike gestures through the window as the engine cuts and the blades throb to a stop. Wild, greasy figures, reminiscent of National Geographic photos of painted cannibals, rush like hungry children to your window. Mike smiles: "They're your brothers and sisters. They'll be seated beside you at the Marriage Feast of the Lamb."

"And today's feast, incidentally," he adds, unbuckling his seat belt, "is marking a new round of baptisms. Saboonwarek, the Pass Valley tribe missionary whose 14 fellow-workers' heads were taken by these people, is doing the baptizing. And the first one to get baptized tomorrow? The head chief. The guy who ordered the massacre. He's now your brother."

Later, during the strange celebration of the feast, you marvel at the power of the Gospel, God's plan to reach every people group with the blessing of redemption. You know that if the 14 Pass Valley martyrs had been Western missionaries, there would be books about them, films, monuments. But here in the remote, primitive highlands of central Irian Jaya, the saga is simply one "incidental" scene in the story of God's plan for the Nipsan.

Here the terror and love of obeying God's command to reach every people seem raw, real. You think of Garrett Khyte handing the ax to that tribesman. You think of Saboonwarek returning to Nipsan, baptizing the chief. You think of the Pass Valley men and their wives and children risking everything, giving their lives so the Nipsan could join them around the throne of the Lamb.

Then you think of self-seeking Christians who are praying about whether or not to put new carpeting into the sanctuary; the medium-size church down the road borrowing from the missions fund to buy a new organ; new buildings; new programs, but little that deals with reaching out to the nations.

Here in Pass Valley, the no-holds-barred obedience to bottom-line responsibility is unnerving. *It makes you wonder if American Christians are even aware of the reality of the spiritual world war raging over the great unchanging purpose of God. Back home, the battle seems so far away, so unrelated to God's global cause. Obedience to God's big-picture mandate is so abstract.*

You're beginning to worry: Are we blind to the realities of God's global drama?

Biblical Revelation

Scripture is clear that God uses blindness. Turn to Isaiah 6:1. "In the year that King Uzziah died, I saw the Lord seated on a throne, high and exalted, and the train of his robe filled the temple."

Isaiah says, "I saw the Lord." With respect to the graph in the last chapter, does this reflect high insight or low insight? High insight. Very high insight, close to "mega-insight"!

"I saw the Lord...holy, holy, holy, is the Lord Almighty." Look at the next verse, verse 4. "At the sound of their voices the door posts and thresholds shook and the temple was filled with a sweet aroma."

Objection! That is not what the Word of God says. Yet, think about it. If you were to envision the Lord standing there, wouldn't it be nice to have a sweet aroma filling the room? The fragrance of roses and flowers from all over the earth permeating the air, raising one to a zenith of excitement and joy. That's not what happened to Isaiah. Rather, the room was filled with smoke.

Why smoke? What does it do? It burns your eyes so that you close them, and it obscures your vision. Isaiah's insight was diminished.

Look at verse five. "Praise the Lord, for I caught a glimpse of the living God." Objection! That's not what it says. Actually, Isaiah panicked. "Woe is me...for I am a man of unclean lips, and I live among a people of unclean lips." He knew his insight was off the graph, yet he also knew he was sinful and he was doomed and destined for judgment. This is why it says in the Old Testament, "No man can see God and live" (Exodus 33:20). Too much insight and we're dead, because of our sin.

Notice that God supernaturally takes care of Isaiah's sin. What does God do?

Isaiah continues; "Then I heard the voice of the Lord saying, 'Whom shall I send? And who will go for us?'"

Because the text does not give any hint as to what that "go" is in reference to, we can conclude that it probably was in reference to something that should have already been well known. What could that be? Of course, going out to all the nations, the bottom line of the covenant. So, to whom was God directing this passage? Israel. There is nothing in the text showing that it was directed solely to Isaiah. God is asking who in Israel, His Great Commission people, would go to the nations.

How many respond out of an entire nation? One. Isaiah's humbled voice gulps, "Here am I. Send me!" Not much of a response for a whole nation. In fact, a terrible, disobedient response.

Look at what God says: "Go and tell this people." Now, if God had said, "Go and tell these peoples," He would be telling Isaiah to go and speak to the nations.

But He says, "Go and tell this people," which could very easily mean He's referring to Israel. Why would God want Isaiah to go back and talk to Israel? Because of their tremendously disobedient response.

So, He's saying, "Go back and tell Israel these words." What do you think He'd tell them in response to their disobedience?

He continues in verse 9 and 10: "Be ever hearing, but never understanding; be ever seeing, but never perceiving. Make the heart of this people calloused; make their ears dull and close their eyes."

Through Isaiah, He's telling Israel that because of their tremendous disobedience, He's going to have to give them ears that cannot hear—hear what? God's Word insight. Eyes that cannot see—see what? More insight. In short, a heart that will be calloused to God's Word.

Why are they not going to understand God's Word? Their disobedience to God's call to go to the nations blinded them to further insight. He's limiting their insight by not making them keen to understand God's Word.

Then you read in verse 10 the word *otherwise*. Otherwise what? Otherwise had they said they would go to the nations and help fulfill the bottom line of the covenant "they might see with their eyes, hear with their ears, understand with their hearts, and turn and be healed."

Had they chosen to obey the bottom line of the covenant, God would have given them all the insight in the world (eyes that can see and ears that can hear), because they would not have had to be judged.

Because of Israel's refusal as a nation to go to the people of the world, God blinds them. If He hadn't, their guilt line would have quickly crossed His Line of Grace. He would then have had to judge them by destroying them, which would have hurt His reputation. And His promise to fulfill the bottom line of the covenant would be in jeopardy.

God's blindness was both a judgment and mercy. Had God's wrath come upon them and God destroyed them, future generations would not have come along and the entire people (except for the one or two found righteous) would have been wiped out. That would have been judgment without mercy.

In Isaiah 29:9-12 we read: "Be stunned and amazed, blind yourselves and be sightless; be drunk, but not from wine, stagger, but not from beer. The Lord has brought over you a deep sleep: He has sealed your eyes [the prophets], he has covered your heads [the seers]." These passages suggest low insight.

The Lord is the one actually doing the blinding. Who is blinded? Israel, because they are choosing to be disobedient. "For you [who are being disobedient] this whole vision is nothing but words sealed in a scroll" (verse 11).

If they are only words sealed in a scroll, the readers cannot understand them. It's "Greek" to them (actually Hebrew!)...keeping them less accountable so God doesn't have to judge them and ruin His reputation.

God is dealing with an entire nation here. But for illustration's sake, let's say He applied this blindness principle in your home town church. You're listening to a sermon that leaves you excited, on the edge of your seat. You've been drinking in every word, and the hour has flown by in two seconds. As the last hymn is sung, you're digesting the truths of the sermon; you want to put it into action. You're walking out of church two inches off the carpet.

As you're being jostled through the doorway, you overhear someone say, "That was the most boring sermon I have ever heard in my entire life. I didn't think it would ever end!"

Now, without playing Spiritual Life Committee chairman, do you think that person plans to obey what he heard? Probably not. Now think of the possibility of God's merciful blindness: Because of God's knowledge of that person's future disobedience, God may have blinded him to prevent his understanding that sermon.

Remember, God doesn't throw pearls before swine. To those Israelites who chose to be obedient, God gave insight. For those who chose to be disobedient, the message was like a bunch of meaningless words on a scroll that's not even opened.

Let's look at a third passage, in Isaiah 42.

Speaking of Israel, it says, "Hear, you deaf, look, you blind, and see! Who is blind but my servant, and deaf like the messenger I send? Who is blind like the one committed to me, blind like the servant of the Lord? You have seen many things, but have paid no attention; your ears are open, but you hear nothing" (verses 18-20). Clearly, this is high disobedience.

Look at the next verse. You can almost insert a "therefore." "[Therefore] it pleased the Lord for the sake of His righteousness to make His law great and glorious."

One aspect of God's law being great and glorious is that it is difficult for many to understand. Many people read the Bible and get absolutely nothing out of it. Why would God allow it to be difficult to understand?

Well, think of the reverse. If God's law weren't difficult to understand, many who read it would be held accountable. And if they were choosing to be disobedient, what could the long-term outcome be for them? Judgment.

So with God making the law great and glorious—difficult to understand—upon whom must we be 100% absolutely dependent in order to understand it? God and His Holy Spirit.

And the Holy Spirit determines to whom He is going to give insight into His word based on His knowledge of our future obedience or disobedience.

You should not say to God, "Lord, show me Your will for my life and then I'll determine whether or not I'll follow it." God usually will not show it to you. He wants to first know of your commitment to obedience before He gives you further insight.

Dozens of other passages deal clearly with this topic, such as: "You have neither heard nor understood; from of old your ear has not been open. Well do I know how treacherous you are; you were called a rebel from birth. For my own name's sake [or for my own reputation] I delay my wrath" (Isaiah 48:8-12).

How did God delay His wrath? By bringing a spiritual blindness on Israel, keeping them less accountable. What would happen if He judged them in His wrath? His reputation would be tarnished, and then all the peoples of the earth would not consider His worthiness to be praised. So for the sake of His praise among the Gentile nations, God withholds His wrath by bringing about blindness.

Eyes That Do Not See

Did Jesus acknowledge these principles of blindness?

In Matthew 13, Jesus teaches the parable of the sower. The disciples then pull Him aside and say, "Why do you speak to the people in parables?" (Matthew 13:10). Good question; why didn't Jesus just very clearly spell out His teachings?

Jesus says, "The knowledge of the secrets of the kingdom of heaven has been given to you, but not to them" (Matthew 13:11). Who's the _you_? The disciples. Did they usually choose obedience or disobedience? Obedience.

"But not to them." Who's the _them_? The Jews. Did they usually choose obedience or disobedience? Disobedience.

The "knowledge of the secrets of the kingdom [high insight] has been given to you [who choose obedience], but not to them [who choose disobedience]." Then Jesus goes on. "Whoever has will be given more, and he will have an abundance." Typical of Jesus, He never fills in the blanks. "Lord, whoever has _what_ will be given more of _what_?"

Whoever has a heart for obedience will be given more insight, and he will have insight in abundance.

Notice the next part of the verse, "Whoever does not have, even what he has will be taken away from him" (Matthew 13:12). Whoever does not have a heart for obedience, even the insight he has will be taken away from him.

Have you ever known a strong believer who walks with the Lord and then suddenly falls into sin? If he refuses to repent and clings to that sin, what begins to happen to his heart?

His heart is hardened more and more. Whoever does not have a heart for obedience, even what insight he has will be taken away from him. Based on God's knowledge of our future obedience or disobedience, He acts, and He can withdraw the power of His Spirit from us, which will harden our hearts. This explains what took place with the Pharaoh. When the Pharaoh hardened his heart (Exodus 5:2), God hardened it even further.

Sharpen your vision: Begin to look at even familiar verses with an eye to note the blindness-disobedience, insight-obedience pattern. For instance, notice John 14:21. "Whoever has my commands and obeys them, he is the one who loves me. He who loves me will be loved by my Father, and I too will love him and will show myself to him." Put the first part and the last part together. Whoever obeys Me...I will give him much insight. A direct link between obedience and insight. Of the one to whom much has been given, much is required.

Blindness Today?

Do you think God is still blinding people today? Is it a Jewish phenomenon only, or could it be Christian as well?

Are there whole congregations in your town who are, in all sincerity, engaged in every social activity you can imagine to foster fellowship, but who are not really concerned about the heart of the Gospel? If so, is God blinding them?

Don't get into a judgmental, holier-than-thou stance on this, but imagine what would happen if God took away the blindness affecting many of our churches. What if He showed every church in the Body of Christ everywhere a vision of His great purpose to reach the nations so clearly that they could not disagree with it? He might then have to judge them, because perhaps many of them would not be obedient to the vision.

Think of it. What would happen if God judged all the churches around the world according to their strict obedience to the Great Commission? Zap! Zap! Zap! The earth would be swallowing up little and big congregations of God's people worldwide, and God's very reputation would be ruined. Think what all the non-Christians (along with the Hindus, Muslims,

Buddhists, etc.) considering Jehovah as their God would say. They'd probably respond to God's judgment with "Thank you, I think I'll stick with my own philosophy if that's the way God treats His people!"

Does God judge disobedient believers eventually? Yes, at the judgment seat of Christ (see II Corinthians 5:10, for example). But for now, out of His mercy for His children as well as for non-Christians, God blinds them. They do not gain insight because they do not apply truth already given them.

Yet, before we end, let's think through some other reasons why God might incorporate blindness into His sovereign plan.

Could your parents be blinded? If they are, why didn't God zap them back when they might have been more accountable? Well, had He done that, who wouldn't have come along? You!

Because God knows of future generations that will choose to be obedient, He holds off judgment through blindness.

What might also happen to your parents two or ten years down the road? They might repent and get in on the greatest task on the face of the earth. That could be another reason.

But let's ask an even more personal question. Were you blinded to this material before you read this book?

If so, why is God giving you insight now? Right. God knows of your future obedience. It is not by accident that this book is in your hands and that you are understanding this material. God in all His sovereignty allowed all of this to take place. In allowing it, He is giving us insight into His word because He knows we want to obey Him. The very fact that you are looking for insight means that you are hungering for it. If you hunger for it, you surely want to obey it, so God will open your eyes to understand.

Once you've finished this study, I suppose you're going to love this book and hate it. You're going to love it because now you have greater insight. You're going to hate this study because now you have a tremendous amount of responsibility.

You can't go back. Your life can't ever be the same. God has given you increased insight and you need to be obedient in your response. You need to act on your new insight, getting more and more involved in the thematic backbone of God's Word. If not, months or years down the road this book could be collecting dust as you hastily go about the business of "Christianity." Having forgotten, you will have been blinded to the depth of God's heart for all nations.

"Selah."

For Further Thought

For individual or group study:

• List other ideas new to you from this chapter's discussion.

• List questions raised in this segment of study.

• Scan the chapters, noting especially meaningful references and mark these in your personal study Bible.

• Evaluate your life and see if there are any attitudes of disobedience which may be keeping you from insight.

• See if this statement is true in your life, "I'll go anywhere, do anything, or say anything for God's kingdom." If not, what could the ramifications be?

• List reasons why God might judge America. How could that judgment come?

• Pray for a missionary movement among the Nipsan tribe.

8—The Covenant Kickoff

Finally, an Ephesians 3:20 experience; they messed up your flight to China, and you flew standby first class! Settling into the noticeably larger seat, you give your drink order as you are handed a complimentary copy of USA Today. You adjust the seat backward and begin to browse through the newspaper. After coming out of the heart of Nipsan territory, it's great to read U.S. news again. You begin to drink in the fresh news from around the world territory.

You finally drift into the editorial page. As you scan the page, you come across the headline, "Who Could Have Guessed It?" You chuckle to yourself without even starting the article. "Well, of course God could have; one day, more of the media will realize who He is."

As you breeze through the article, you realize the writer is responding to recent events in Eastern Europe. "It took ten years for Poland to gain its independence. Germany gained it in ten months, Yugoslavia in ten weeks, and Bulgaria in ten days."

You reflect on your time in Albania with Greg Livingstone, as well as on the missions conference held at your church two months ago. East Germany...what did they say was happening there before it was unified with West Germany? "Our mission agency was offered one million dollars to pass out tracts on the East German border. We turned it down because 30 million tracts had already been distributed since the Wall came down. That is three tracts for every man, woman, and child in East Germany....An Eastern European country has given us a building to start a Bible school for its people. They are coming to us. We have also totally depleted our stockpile of Bibles, which in a matter of days was dispersed among the peoples throughout this Eastern country. Romania already has a Romanian Missionary Alliance, and Far East Broadcasting Company (FEBC) is hoping to set up a Christian radio station within the country."

"Boy," you think to yourself, "God is really doing something in Eastern Europe."

"Here's your Diet Sprite with a twist of lime," the flight attendant says, interrupting your thoughts. Sipping on your drink, you continue to scan the article now commenting about the new Commonwealth of Independent States that replaced the former Soviet Union.

"Oh, yes," you think to yourself. "Didn't my college room-mate tell me that even when they were still the Soviet Union, they had invited some major Christian student groups to begin work on their college campuses and show the Jesus film to all of their students? The FEBC had reported receiving 4,000 letters from the Soviet Union in one week! And aren't they now printing Bibles in the Commonwealth, though before they wouldn't even let them in? And aren't the Christians there starting their own missionary sending agencies? Wow, God is really doing something exciting!"

With no rhyme or reason, you begin thinking about China and Tienanmen Square. "Didn't one of the missionaries tell me that more intellectuals have come to know Christ since Tienanmen Square than in the previous ten years in China? Didn't another say that more Chinese are open to the Gospel since that event than in any of the previous years that he had been there?

"Wait a second," you think to yourself. "Of course God could have guessed it, but did God plan it?"

Your mind begins to race. "Could God be arranging these major events in history to bring about His purposes here on the earth? Did He use Iraq's invasion of Kuwait for His purposes? Are all these major events linked to each other? Are they happening because of God's promise to Abraham?"

Linking the Major Events Toward His Goal

If the Abrahamic Covenant is the thematic backbone of all Scripture, then you would think that most of the major events in the Bible would somehow hinge on that promise. That's exactly what happens. Let's see how this kicks off in the Old Testament.

Did you ever wonder why God said to Abraham, "Abe, I'm going to give you all of this land, but you can't have it right now. You are going to have to go away for 400 years of captivity before you can have it"?

The answer is found in Genesis 34. Dinah had been violated by Shechem of the Hivite tribe. Because of his love for her, he wanted to marry her. He asked permission from her father, and was willing to pay any bride price. Notice her family's response: "Because their sister Dinah had been defiled, Jacob's sons replied deceitfully as they spoke to Shechem and his father Hamor. They said to them, 'We can't do such a thing; we can't give our sister to a man who is not circumcised. That would be a disgrace to us. We will give our consent to you on one condition only: that you become like us by circumcising all your males. Then we will give you our daughters and take your daughters for ourselves. We'll settle among you and become one people with you. But if you will not agree to be circumcised, we'll take our sister and go.'"

Notice the latter part of the response. What could have happened to the descendants of Abraham and the Shechemites? They could have become "one people"! What would that have meant to the distinct tribe of Abraham? It would have been lost, scattered through co-mingling with nation after nation. Why didn't God just allow Abraham to stay in that land and grow and multiply?

Abraham's descendants were living among peoples with a similar cultural background. Because they were not that distinct, it was quite possible for the Israelites to intermarry with other people groups and lose their ethnicity.

If any of these had been the result, the promise God made to Abraham could not be fulfilled, because it was made to Abraham and His descendants. If their ethnicity had been lost, the covenant would have been lost. God needed a common task to keep them as a distinct ethnic group. But notice one other thing. Jacob's sons replied "deceitfully." They weren't telling the truth. Why? What happened? You've read the rest of the story; they killed the Shechemites. What did that do to their reputation, and their God's reputation? "Uhmmm, boy, don't trust those Israelites or their God! They're not to be messed with."

With this type of a reputation, what nation would want to follow the God of Israel? We've seen this before through Moses! Notice what Jacob said. "Then Jacob said to Simeon and Levi, 'You have brought trouble on me by making me a stench to the Canaanites and Perizzites, the people living in this land. We are few in number, and if they join forces against me and attack me, I and my household will be destroyed.' But they replied, 'Should he have treated our sister like a prostitute?'" (Genesis 34:30,31). They could have been destroyed by any other nation avenging the Shechemite incident. So in order to erase a bad reputation over time and save the ethnicity of His people, God sent them into 400 years of Egyptian captivity. God specifically wanted to make them a great nation in Egypt (Genesis 46:3). Why Egypt?

There are many reasons. The first deals with the broad cultural differences between the Egyptians and the Hebrews. The Egyptians were polytheistic rulers, and the Hebrews were monotheistic slaves. This in itself made the Hebrew people reject the Egyptian culture, and thus the Hebrews would never intermarry with the Egyptians on a large scale. Also, the Egyptians protected the Hebrew people politically. Under Egyptian protection, they were allowed to grow and multiply greatly (Exodus 1:7). As a result, the Hebrew people were not destroyed in the Promised Land by any group going on a rampage, possibly trying to revenge the Shechemite incident.

The 400 years that transpired between the time of Joseph's entering Egypt and the Exodus also allowed the sin of the Amorites to reach its "fullness." What does fullness mean with respect to our graph on blindness? Judgment. It took 400 years of the Amorites' sin to become so great that God chose to act on His hatred for sin, bringing about His judgment.

Another reason God may have put Israel under Egyptian captivity was that He wanted to use the Exodus to establish His reputation throughout all the earth. Remember the plagues? The Red Sea? All of these miraculous events allowed God's reputation to be established. In Exodus 5:1-2, we find out that God's reputation had not been established prior to these events.

The Promised Land

As God took the Hebrews out of Egypt, He placed them back in the Promised Land. We already know the Promised Land was a very strategic piece of property, but there is more to it than that. As the sin of the Amorites had reached its fullness, God had the Hebrew people retake the Promised Land by destroying all the other nations. That seems to show that A > B, but we know that it's not. If you look at it through an A = B set of lenses, God's destruction of all those nations came about because their guilt line had crossed God's Line of Grace and He was bringing about judgment as he would have with any nation. It just so happened that God was using the Hebrew people to bring about that judgment.

This helps answer the age-old question, "How could a loving God destroy so many people in the Old Testament?" It wasn't done as an A > B vengeful act; rather it was an A = B holy act, destroying the tremendous wickedness of the nations in the Promised Land.

The Kingdom Divided

Later, the nation of Israel had three kings in the Promised Land who, good or bad, held the people together as one nation: Saul, David, and Solomon. God replaced Saul, a bad king, with David. God replaced good King David with his son Solomon. Solomon started out as a good king, but strayed. And with whom did God replace him? Two kings; God divided the kingdom.

Now, why didn't God do with Solomon as He had done with Saul? God could have replaced Solomon with his son. Instead, He divided the kingdom. There must have been some reason beyond personal disobedience such as seen in Saul, that caused God to completely split the kingdom of His chosen people.

Remembering that every major event in the story of the Bible hinges on the Abrahamic Covenant and has top-line and bottom-line ramifications, let's think through God's rationale for dividing the nation.

First Kings 11 tells us that Solomon had "seven hundred wives of royal birth and three hundred concubines....As Solomon grew old, his wives turned his heart after other gods, and his heart was not fully devoted to the Lord his God, as the heart of David his father had been. He followed Ashtoreth, the goddess of the Sidonians, and Molech the detestable god of the Ammonites...

"On a hill east of Jerusalem, Solomon built a high place for Chemosh the detestable god of Moab, and for Molech the detestable god of the Ammonites. He did the same for all his foreign wives, who burned incense and offered sacrifices to their gods" (I Kings 11:3-8). Solomon had hundreds of wives of foreign descent: Ammonites, Hittites, the Pharaoh's daughter, and on and on. And they were all probably homesick!

If you've ever been overseas for more than a year, what's the greatest thing you can get from home? Food? No. Mail, right? There's nothing like hearing about what's happening in the homeland.

Solomon had a household full of foreign correspondents who regularly passed news on to their families, their friends, their own people groups. And how did they find out about what was happening at home? By listening for their homeland dialects down in the marketplace. By catching up on news from travelers and passing message packets to traders coming through Jerusalem, the world trade-route center.

What do you think these wives told the traders from their homelands? "Hey, go back and tell our people that Solomon is beginning to worship our gods. The God of Israel is *passe!*"

As the traders would plod into or stride out of Jerusalem, what did they see that would authenticate the news? High on the mountain east of Jerusalem were temples to other gods. God's reputation was being destroyed. So what did God do?

He could have turned the nation over to Solomon's son Rehoboam. But read through I Kings 12 to realize that God's reputation would only have suffered more degradation among the nations because Rehoboam was a terrible king. Had he taken over everything his father owned, he really would have destroyed

God's reputation. Disobedience that affects the name of God, that threatens the fulfillment of the bottom line of God's promise to every people group, is always followed by judgment. Hence God divided the kingdom, another major event hinging on the Abrahamic Covenant.

Dispersion

Israel was special, but God's equal commitment was to spread His Name to all the nations.

Actually, at no time did God's love for Israel get in the way of His commitment to His own reputation and thus His glory among the nations. To God, A is not greater than B. He was willing to divide the kingdom and allow His people to eventually go into captivity for the sake of His reputation among the earth's peoples.

Listen to God's heart: "It is not for your sake, O house of Israel, that I am going to do these things, but for the sake of my holy name, which you have profaned among the nations where you have gone. I will show the holiness of my great name...the name you have profaned among them. Then the nations will know that I am the Lord, declares the Sovereign Lord, when I show myself holy through you before their eyes" (Ezekiel 36:22-23).

God wants to evangelize all the world, to fulfill His top-line/bottom-line purposes. But His people were being disobedient. They were so wrapped up in themselves that they forgot to be obedient to the bottom line and were even missing out on the top line! So God said He was going to scatter them like a whirlwind among the nations (Zechariah 7:13-14).

In Ezekiel 5:12 we find that a third of them died from the plague, a third of them died from the sword, and the last third got dispersed to the nations as God's judgment struck this disobedient group. Notice the irony of the passage from Isaiah that begins this chapter. God uses the nations, the very people groups Israel is to be blessing, to carry out His judgment.

While in captivity, the third who were dispersed repented. And, naturally, they then became a witness to the nations. Remember the testimonies of Daniel, Shadrach, Meshach, and Abednego? God, in His sovereignty, will reach every people with the blessing of redemption, and since the Israelites wouldn't go to the nations, He sent them to the nations through the Babylonian and Assyrian captivities. He brought down two birds with one stone: their judgment and world evangelization!

It was God's involuntary "go" mechanism.

The effects were incredible; even King Nebuchadnezzar repented and proclaimed that everyone in his Babylonian kingdom was to follow and worship the God of the Jews.

Imagine: You're one of the other nations conquered by the great Nebuchadnezzar, and you read his order to worship a non-Babylonian god. For years you've heard the rumors about Nebuchadnezzar being reduced to the state of a mindless beast by this god—he was crazy for seven years. Now he's in his right mind, and he's issuing orders to worship the god of the Jews, God Most High. Perhaps you'll follow orders. First, you need to find a local Jew and ask about this God: Who is He? How do we worship Him? What are the basic beliefs?

There will be people—Egyptians, Babylonians, etc.—who acknowledge Him, even if God has to use the disobedience of His people. The main events continue to be linked together.

Homecoming

After 70 years of captivity, God orders His people back to rebuild the walls of Jerusalem: "I will bring health and healing to it [Jerusalem]; I will heal my people and will let them enjoy abundant peace and security. I will bring back Judah and Israel from captivity and will rebuild them as they were before. I will cleanse them from all the sin they have committed against me and will forgive all their sins of rebellion against me" (Jeremiah 33:6-8).

That sounds like the top line, and since we know that with every top-line blessing comes a bottom-line responsibility, let's look at the next verse to see if the bottom line is there as well. "Then this city will bring me renown, joy, praise and honor before all nations on earth..." (Jeremiah 33:9).

For Such a Time as This

Some of His people, though, never journeyed back to the Promised Land after the time of the captivity. After 70 years in Babylon/Medo-Persia, the Jews probably had their own schools set up. They had developed kosher-food distribution systems; they had their own little forms of government. So they stayed. Did God use this?

The book of Esther dramatizes the circumstances of those Hebrews who stayed in the lands of their captivity. Remember the basic story? Esther becomes queen of the Medo-Persian Empire at exactly the right time to intercede in behalf of her Hebrew people.

If you have an A > B perspective, what was God doing as Queen Esther saved her people? He was simply protecting them from their enemies. But if you have an A = B perspective, several events of this wonderful story take on new significance, such as the gala ending: "In every province and in every city, wherever the edict of the king went, there was joy and gladness among the Jews, with feasting and celebrating. And many people of other nationalities became Jews because the fear of the Jews had seized them" (Esther 8:17).

Notice the geography involved: every province, every city in the kingdom which stretched from India to Ethiopia (Esther 1:1)! Individuals from all sorts of people groups in the Medo-Persian empire converted to Judaism. And in all probability there were many more who did not actually become Jews but who did decide to fear the God of Israel.

These "God-fearing Gentiles" passed that attitude on from generation to generation. It was that event, through Esther, that set the stage for the apostle Paul's evangelism to spread like wildfire. Notice the term "God-fearing" Gentiles many times in the Scriptures (Acts 10:2,22; 13:26,50; 17:4,17).

So God used even Israel's disobedience and dispersion to fulfill the bottom line of the covenant. He said, "I will display my glory among the nations, and all the nations will see the punishment I inflict and the hand I lay upon them. From that day forward the house of Israel will know that I am the Lord their

God. And the nations will know that the people of Israel went into exile for their sin, because they were unfaithful to me" (Ezekiel 39:21-23). God upheld His name among the nations.

Do you see how these major events of Hebrew history in Scripture hinge on God's desire to fulfill His promise to Abraham and to reach both Jews and Gentiles? And those events shape a story with a single theme: a theme that gives us a clear sense of God's historic purpose, a theme stating a clear priority for our lives bringing God greater glory by winning representatives from every tongue, tribe, and nation!

Did you know that God is still in control of the major events in today's world?

God's love for the Iranians was so great that back in the '70s, He "kicked" all the missionaries out by allowing one man to take power: the Ayatollah Khomeini. (Remember that Romans 13:1 says that all leaders of the governments are appointed by God.)

Exercising his powers, the Ayatollah began taking his nation back to the basics of the Koran. In so doing, Islamic law reigned.

As he lived out what he felt to be the Koranic way, he publicly executed those who did not agree with his laws. He even took 10-year-old boys, placed a plastic key to heaven around their necks, and put them in the front lines of the army. The boys were told that if they were killed, they would be guaranteed entrance into heaven. They were then instructed to march across mine fields to allow the army to follow on unmined territory.

As the average Iranian saw this happen, he got so disgusted with the Ayatollah and his ways that he said, "If this is Islam, I want nothing to do with it!" Since the Ayatollah took power, more Iranians came into Christ's Kingdom than in all the history of missions to Iran.

God is still in charge of today's major events and He's currently writing new chapters in Church history—with or without us.

Did you realize that the officials of the former Soviet Union had such a distaste for Christians in their army that they wanted them all killed off? What was their strategy? They put Christians in the front lines of their battles.

Was God still in control? Yes! As the Christians were sent to the front lines in the war with Afghanistan, many were not killed, but instead shared with the Muslims about Christ. Reports are now coming out about Muslims who came to know Christ through the witnessing of Soviet soldiers. God is still in control!

The falling of the Iron Curtain showed the imprint of God's hand, as well. Today, Campus Crusade for Christ is taking the film *Jesus* openly into the schools of the former Soviet Union and teaching about the life of Christ at the request of the government!

Kazakhstan, a part of the Commonwealth of Independent States, is actively seeking better relations with the West, allowing many Christians to go into the country as tentmakers!

Albania, once considered the hardest country of the world to get into, is now wide open for the Gospel—and ripe!

Desert Storm opened up new avenues for Christians to get into the Middle East. This has also caused many Iraqis to inquire about Christ and Christianity, and has also brought the Kurds to the attention of the Church worldwide. With the prayers and relief efforts going to the Kurds, there are now reports of some 250 Kurdish villages in which new churches have been established.

It's being reported now that there are up to 1,000 Saudis who came to know the Lord as a result of the Gulf War. The Church in Kuwait had only around 50 people meeting prior to the War, and are now reporting up to 500! The government of Iraq broadcasted Campus Crusade's film *Jesus* over national TV.

If you want to see what God is doing, read the newspaper. His hand is there. Although He may wear gloves and not leave fingerprints, He is still in control of the major events in this world. Trust in that!

For Further Thought

For individual or group study:

* List ideas new to you from this chapter's discussion.
* List questions raised in this segment of study.
* Scan the chapter, noting especially meaningful references, and marking these in your Bible.
* List the major events covered in this chapter and, from memory, show how they relate to the Abrahamic Covenant.
* As if you were preparing an open-book quiz for a class, write out five key questions on the material in this chapter. Then be sure you could answer them from memory!
* Read the headlines of today's news, and see how God is behind them.
* Pray that God will raise up laborers quickly to fulfill His promise to Abraham.

9—The Second Half

You're still spinning around the world on a trip that unnerves you. You're tired. This is your last stop. But you know it's a big world, and there are still thousands of unreached people groups you haven't even seen or heard of.

So as you barrel along the main highway skirting the foothills of the Himalayas in a Jeep without a muffler, you try not to think about how many lost there are among the millions and millions of individuals in the People's Republic of China (PRC) alone.

The area is red-earthed and rocky. Bucolic views of valleys appear around every other corner as the Jeep squeals along the last curvy stretch of paved highway before entering Naxiland in the Lijiang Valley in northwestern Yunan Province. Your official government guide tells you this has long been a hub of trade between Yunan and Tibet.

You've heard the remarkable statistic that there are about 50 million believers in China right now. But you know most of those Christians are ensconced in the Han Chinese majority culture and are not necessarily targeting the minority people groups within their borders.

Here in the southwestern corner of China, Yunan Province is home to 24 distinct ethnic groups, most of whom won't be reached through typical, near-neighbor evangelism.

One of these 24 is the Naxi (NAW-shee) people.

You hang on as the Jeep hurtles onto a dirt and gravel road; and in the cool, dry air you review your unofficial notes cribbed from various China-watching groups back home:

- *Naxi, Population: 240,000*
- *Language: Similar to Tibetan. There is no written language, yet they once used a pictograph system for religious writings. Although they cling stubbornly to their ethnic traditions, many Naxi now also speak*

Mandarin, the language of the majority Han Chinese.
*   *Social structure: The Naxi people live in compact*
    communities. Due to the influence of matriarchal social
    traditions, Naxi women occupy the important roles in
    Naxi agriculture and horse-breeding. Living in large
    households ruled by the grandmother, Naxi women
    handle business affairs while the men play a domestic
    role, caring for the children and tending the garden.

A Naxi couple lives with the woman's family. She may have
more than one husband, or she may share her sister's husband
or husbands in a sort of group marriage. Marriage relationships
are very informal: A young woman takes a man as a partner for
several months, or years, or a few days. There is little concept of
close relationship between father and child.

The official PRC line is, of course, that the Chinese people
are one. They are simply called "The People." However, as you
drive by road-construction sites and sporadic rustic houses, you
see that the various people groups are definitely distinct, even in
their dress. You see more Naxi women along the roadside.

They wear traditional costumes of gray homespun pleated
skirts, and capes which are dark blue above and white below,
with a row of seven tasseled disks across the back which glint in
the bright, high altitude sunlight. The elements of this "firma-
ment cape" represent the heavens. The blue symbolizes the night
sky, the white is for daytime, and the seven disks represent stars.

This quaint reminder of the Naxi link to nature is sullied as
you glance at your notes on Naxi religion as your Jeep roars into
the outskirts of a small town. The Naxi worship nature gods in a
mixture of Tibetan Lamanism and the ancient Bon religion,
Buddhism, Chinese Taoism, and spiritism. Their many gods and
demons are placated and manipulated with magic and elaborate
rituals involving blood sacrifices. Naxi shamans invite the gods
or demons to possess them, and, while in a trance, they foretell
the future and answer questions. Most of the gods are portrayed
as fierce and terrible as they trample on animals or humans.
Among the most fearsome gods is Yama, the god of death. His

partner, Tsamundi, a goddess, is often portrayed as holding a skull-bowl full of blood. The Naxi are lifelong captives of fear.

You pull into a market area in the little town where several caped Naxi, tossing trayfuls of large purple beans into the air, are winnowing the husks and singing together. In its simple exotica, the town isn't much of a reminder that you're entering a region held in bondage for thousands of years by the satanic god of death, Yama.

As the noise of the Jeep finally dies and you step down on Naxi ground, the thought of being with one of only two or three known Naxi Christians in this quarter-million people group makes you shiver.

Isaiah 49:25 is, as it has been throughout your journey through the remote hinterlands of China, your consolation: "The prey of the terrible [Yama] will be delivered" (KJV).

You again pray in God's will that Satan's age-old domination over this people group will be broken, and you beseech the Lord of the harvest to send out laborers into His harvest (see Luke 10:2) to bring foreign or Han Chinese Christians into Naxiland. What could the message of Jesus Christ do here? If He were on the earth, would an obscure place like the Lijiang Valley be His ministry base? Would He bother with ethnic minorities?

Jesus' Ministry to Ethnic Minorities

"When Jesus had heard that John had been put in prison, he returned to Galilee. Leaving Nazareth, he went and lived in Capernaum" (Matthew 4:12,13). Jesus based His ministry in Capernaum. Many Jews will say that Jesus was not the Messiah because He didn't headquarter His ministry in Jerusalem, the heart of Judaism. This is said with what kind of a perspective? You guessed it, A > B.

Some of the people around Capernaum spoke Latin, some in Decapolis spoke Greek, and in Capernaum most citizens spoke Hebrew. There was a distinctive mixture of Jewish and Gentile influences. Why did Jesus choose Capernaum rather than Jerusalem?

Matthew writes, "Jesus went throughout Galilee, teaching in

their synagogues, preaching the good news of the kingdom, and healing every disease and sickness among the people. News about him spread all over Syria" (Matthew 4:23-24). Was Syria a Jewish or Gentile area? Does Scripture say: "And the people brought to him were ill with various diseases...And He healed the Jews and He sent the Gentiles home"? Obviously not. He healed "them," Jew and Gentile alike. And as they skipped and praised their way home, what do you think those Gentiles were talking about? This Jesus, this Man who has power to heal.

Why base His ministry in Capernaum? Because Jesus could have immediate contact with a whole spectrum of people groups. A = B. So "large crowds from Galilee, the Decapolis, Jerusalem, Judea and the region across the Jordan followed him" (Matthew 4:25). Not only that, but He also knew that Jews south in Jerusalem had enough motivation to move north and check out a possible Messiah, whereas Gentiles from Syria probably wouldn't have had enough motivation to take the long journey south to see a miracle worker.

There are plenty of simple passages in the New Testament describing Jesus' heart for all humanity. And there are many excellent commentaries on the Gospels' references to the Gentiles (any peoples that are non-Jewish). So rather than studying these familiar passages, let's take a quick look at some of those New Testament passages that seem to suggest A > B, that Jesus did not come to minister to the Gentiles but to the Jews only.

For example, as He sends out the Twelve, He says, "Do not go among the Gentiles or enter any town of the Samaritans. Go rather to the lost sheep of Israel. As you go, preach this message: 'The kingdom of heaven is near'" (Matthew 10:5-7).

So much for the premise of our study together, right? If He were a whole-covenant Messiah, both top and bottom line, how could He possibly order them to "not go among the Gentiles"?

Let's fast-forward for a moment to the events of Acts 11. Jesus has lived His life on this earth, risen from the dead, told the disciples to reach all peoples. Now, after much time has passed, "the apostles and the brothers throughout Judea heard that the

Gentiles also had received the word of God" (Acts 11:1).

But notice verses 2 and 3. "So when Peter went up to Jerusalem, the circumcised believers criticized him and said, 'You went into the house of uncircumcised men and ate with them.'" Translated: "Peter, you're our leader; how could you do this? We're going to have to start the impeachment proceedings." They obviously weren't too happy.

Yet, once Peter reviewed the events of the conversion of Cornelius, they "had no further objections and praised God, saying, 'So then, God has granted even the Gentiles repentance unto life'" (Acts 11:18). As if it were something brand new!

If, at this later point, the disciples were still so squeamish and reticent to share their faith with Gentiles, how much more did they have that same perspective at the beginning of the ministry of Jesus? Skip back to Matthew 10.

Can you imagine the disciples swimming across the Jordan and telling the Gentiles, "Hey, you Gentiles, guess what. God loves you and has a wonderful plan for your life." The Gentiles would look at each other and then jump up with excitement, exclaiming, "God loves us? That's terrific. Can we hug you?"

Of course the disciples, being firmly entrenched in an A > B theology, would reply, "Don't touch us, you Gentile dogs!"

"Oh well, at least come into our homes and get warmed by the fire. You must be cold, as you're so wet."

"No, we're not allowed into Gentile homes; it's against our religion."

"Well, can we feed you? You must be hungry," they'd reply in trying to help those who had brought them such "good news."

"No," the disciples would retort. "We brought our own kosher lunches...."

Would it have been good news at that point? No.

It is as if Jesus said, "Look, gentlemen, you've got such an A > B perspective that you'll ruin any attempt to reach the Gentiles. Just go to the Jews for now and try to get this message straight. Later I'll send you to the Gentiles."

He's very clear about this "later" idea: "On my account you will be brought before governors and kings as witnesses to them and to the Gentiles" (Matthew 10:18). He seems to be telling them He'll send them to the Gentiles once they get the message down pat: the theme of God's blessing of redemption.

Notice in Luke 10:1-16 that Jesus later sends out the 72 (which the NIV says could be translated as 70). Whereas Jesus had sent out the 12 and instructed them not to go to the Gentiles, now He sends out the 70 and simply says for them to go to everyone.

Now, those numbers, 12 and 70, could be symbolic: 12 can represent the 12 tribes while 70 can represent the nations. Regardless, this later commissioning makes it obvious that the earlier injunction to go only to the Jews was a temporary top-line mandate. When He sent out the 70, he gave the parallel bottom-line mandate.

The Canaanite Woman

Let's think through the classic passage some use to suggest that Jesus wanted no dealings with anyone but Jews. Read through Matthew 15:21-28:

> A Canaanite woman from that vicinity came to him, crying out, "Lord, Son of David, have mercy on me! My daughter is suffering terribly from demon-possession."

Jesus did not answer a word.

So his disciples came to him and urged him, "Send her away, for she keeps crying out after us."

He answered, "I was sent only to the lost sheep of Israel." The woman came and knelt before him. "Lord, help me!" she said. He replied, "It is not right to take the children's bread and toss it to their dogs." "Yes, Lord," she said, "but even the dogs eat the crumbs that fall from their masters' table."

Then Jesus answered, "Woman, you have great faith! Your request is granted." And her daughter was healed from that very hour.

How do we align this passage with the rest of the Bible's top-line/bottom-line, A = B theology? Very simply. Get a pair of scissors, cut the passage out, and all the Scripture will be harmonious. A = B. No problem.

Seriously, analyze this unusual story. Look at it in its context. Turn to the beginning of Matthew 15. Here Jesus begins to speak about what is clean and what is unclean, the outside of the cup versus the inside, that it is what is on the inside of the heart that makes a man clean or unclean. In other words, it doesn't matter whether you're a Jew or a Gentile on the outside, what matters is what's in your heart. He was giving them an A = B lesson! It's very clear.

But His disciples have what kind of a perspective? A > B.

Notice (Matthew 15:21) that Jesus then leaves that Jewish area and purposely withdraws to the region of Tyre and Sidon, a Gentile area. Why does He do that? You guessed it; He wants to run into Gentiles. Once they arrive, however, a Gentile woman confronts Jesus, and He remains silent. Why?

Perhaps Jesus does not offer a word to the woman because He wants to test His disciples' understanding of His recent lesson. Have they learned their lesson? Obviously not: "Send her away," they say, "for she keeps crying out after us." It's as if they were saying, "It's about time You gave us a chance to speak up. Thanks for not saying a word; Lord, we'd really like to enforce this idea that Your love for the Jews is far greater than for all the nations, those Gentile dogs. Let's just send her on her way."

So Jesus, in effect, said, "Look, there goes your A > B perspective again. Okay, is that the game you want to play? For the next few moments I'll live it out the way you want it to be lived out." So He tells the woman, "I'm sorry, but I was sent only to the lost sheep of Israel."

Notice her response: "Lord, help me," she says.

He replies, "It's not right to take the children's bread and toss it to the dogs." Can you believe this? Jesus called her a dog! He obviously hadn't read Dale Carnegie's book, *How To Win Friends and Influence People.* Was using that discriminatory slang a healthy thing to do in Gentile Tyre? Probably not, if you want to start a worldwide movement. He is obviously stressing some point.

And think through what He is saying: "It's not right to take the children's bread and toss it to the dogs." The term *children* represents what people? The Jews. *Bread* represents what? The blessing. It's not right to take Israel's blessing and toss it to the dogs, the Gentiles.

Is that true or false? False. It goes in direct opposition to the entire Old Testament's emphasis on top-line and bottom-line theology. Jesus here purposely misquotes the Abrahamic Covenant! If Jesus is not speaking satirically, He is revising the Abrahamic Covenant on the spot! But this He cannot do without perjuring the Godhead, since Genesis 22:16-18 and Hebrews 6:13-18 reveal that God had bound Himself by an unchanging oath to fulfill both requirements of that sacred covenant.

Why would Jesus misquote such a basic teaching? Why does Jesus call the Gentiles dogs? Why does He say, "I was sent only to the lost sheep of Israel"? Perhaps because He is trying to teach His disciples something, to play the game of the disciples by acting out the A > B philosophy and demonstrating how far it could go. Somehow, maybe through the twinkle of His eye, Jesus nonverbally communicates to that woman, "Woman, hang in there. I'm trying to give my disciples an illustration of a lesson I just taught." Jesus keeps the woman coming back. Then as the Greek text hints, He turns (as if His back had been to her the whole time) and says, "Woman, you have great faith." Her daughter is healed.

It may be at this point in the role-playing exercise that Peter turns to James and says, "We've been had; He meant to heal her the whole time."

After Jesus went from Tyre to Sidon, He came back to the other side of the Sea of Galilee (Gentile area) and fed the 4,000. Earlier, He had fed the 5,000 Jews. When He comes to the feeding of the mainly Gentile crowd of 4,000, He says to the disciples, "Get them some food." Their response? "Lord, there's no way You can feed these people. How can we find food in this remote place?" Remote place? They were in Gentile territory. They were very uncomfortable. Now, they had just seen Jesus feed 5,000 men with their women and children. All He was asking them to do was to feed 4,000 men with their families, and they're basically saying, "It can't be done."

Why can't it be done? Probably because they figured that God would never feed Gentiles miraculously. But Jesus, being a whole-covenant Messiah, feeds the 5,000 Jews—top line—and then the 4,000 Gentiles—bottom line. He is a whole-covenant Messiah, fulfilling the whole law.

These major events are still revolving around the Abrahamic Covenant, making this promise foundational both in the New Testament and in the lives of believers today!

Mike Rogers of Houston, Texas is one such individual. He is an engineer and makes $42,000 annually. He is single, living with another single guy in downtown Houston. They share expenses on a house that rents for $350 per month. Mike currently gives away 40 percent of his income, and plans to give 44 percent when he gets an expected raise.

Mike didn't start out this way. When he graduated from college, he went on a two-month mission trip with Youth With A Mission. At that time he began feeling that the Lord was calling him to be a "sender" rather than a "go-er."

After starting his job, Mike took the "Perspectives on the World Christian Movement" course in the Houston area. This course opened his eyes to the priority of the bottom line. Though Mike was already committed to paying off a debt, he began giving away 20 percent of his gross income. Ten percent went to his local church, and ten percent went to other needy programs. Each year Mike has been able to increase his giving.

Mike used to "scatter" his gifts broadly to various people, but now he has a more focused plan of giving. When I first met him, I challenged Mike to get involved with adopting a people group. Now he is a firm supporter of one of the teams within Frontiers. He gives $200 monthly to this team, but his commitment doesn't stop there.

As Mike gained a vision for supporting a team, he began to challenge others to do the same. He mapped out his own strategy and asked three other young men to join him. Last year they gave $4,000 to this specific project. They still make that investment and are taking on new areas to support.

Rick and Satoko Hill have seen the priority of the bottom line in their lives. They have chosen to make God's heart for the world the major theme of their lives.

Rick has his own computer consulting business. After considering their needs, Rick and Satoko have made a commitment to live on $2,500 monthly. Rick makes $60,000-$80,000 annually in his business. This means that they give away over 50 percent of his income.

Rick and Satoko live in a nice, three-bedroom house which is paid for. They enjoy two weeks of vacation each year and have substantial savings for emergencies. They feel that they have a good living on the limited income they have set for themselves.

Rick tithes ten percent of his $2,500 "living allowance" to his church, then gives anything over that allowance to missions through his church or directly to individuals or agencies. As a family, the Hills know that they are contributing significantly to establishing God's Kingdom on this earth by sending others.

The Abrahamic Covenant *is* foundational in the Scriptures from Genesis to Revelation. Being the central theme of the Scriptures, shouldn't it be the main driving theme of our lives? "Selah."

For Further Thought

For individual or group study:

- Scan the chapter, noting especially meaningful references and marking these in your personal study Bible.
- List the past three major events in your own life. Ask yourself the question, "Was there any bottom-line involvement there?"
- Think through the next three significant events in your life. How will the bottom line be involved?
- Spend five minutes in prayer for the Naxi unreached people of Yunan Province in China.

10—A Checkup for the Church

We have seen major events in the story of the Bible hinging on God's desire to reach all the nations. God's promise to Abraham is foundational in the Word...even for today. Now let's get even more practical and personal. If God has commissioned us to reach every distinct ethnic group on the face of the earth, how are we doing?

If a profit-oriented, multi-national corporation were given this challenge of reaching every distinct ethnic group with a sales offer, they'd have tremendous plans, goals, and projections; they'd know where there was progress; they'd know where they were going in five years, in ten years, and so on.

Unfortunately, we as the Body of Christ have faltered in our planning, in our objectives, in tracking God's progress in this global project. We don't know where we're going. So it's time to assess where we are with the Gospel, how we're doing, and what our goals are to reach the nations.

The Picture is Encouraging!

First, let's highlight part of a passage we've looked at earlier in our study: "When God made his promise to Abraham...he swore by himself, saying, 'I will surely bless you and give you many descendants'...Because God wanted to make the unchanging nature of his purpose very clear to the heirs of what was promised, he confirmed it with an oath. God did this so that, by two unchangeable things in which it is impossible for God to lie, we who have fled to take hold of the hope offered to us may be greatly encouraged" (Hebrews 6:13-18).

One of the objectives of our study of God's big picture is that you be greatly encouraged. God is going to finish this task. He is going to reach the nations, and you can be a significant part of that process. Perhaps through this study you're catching an awareness that your life can be riveted with purpose and drive in a cause that is eternally significant.

Now, focus on the little phrase in Hebrews 6:17—"the unchanging nature of his purpose." If the ceiling were to blow off the building where you now sit reading so diligently, if the heavens were to open up wide and you were to see God and say, "Lord, what is it that's on Your heart right now?" based on His Word, we know that His response would be something like this: "I love you and want to bless you. And I want you to turn around and be a blessing to the nations, because I want every group of people on the face of this earth to know My love." What's on His heart is unchanging.

You're blessed to be a blessing. He meant it when He said it at the time of Abraham. He meant it at the time of David. He meant it at the time of Ezekiel. He meant it at the time of Jesus. He meant it in Count Zinzendorf's time with the Moravians. And He means it now. It's His unchanging purpose, and He wants to make it very, very clear...to you.

Blessing all the world's people groups with salvation is the sum of the unchanging nature of God's purpose. We are co-workers with God in that endeavor.

Since this is His unchanging nature, how are we doing?

Record of the Unreached Peoples

World population has fluctuated from 70 distinct ethnic groups after the tower of Babel, to 60,000 people groups at the time of Christ, down to approximately 24,000 distinct ethnic groups today. About 12,000 of these ethnic groups have been reached; they have a church movement within their culture that is capable of evangelizing its own people group.

Yet that means there are another 12,000 people groups who have not had their first chance to say "yes" or "no" to Jesus' love for them; 2.4 billion people who have no one in their culture who speaks their language, who could tell them about the good news of our Lord...one out of every two people on the face of the earth. Study through the following chart of the world's proportions of believers and non-Christians who live in a culture where they can find out about the Gospel. Then notice the non-Christians in unreached people groups who do not have an honest chance to say "yes" or "no" to Jesus Christ.

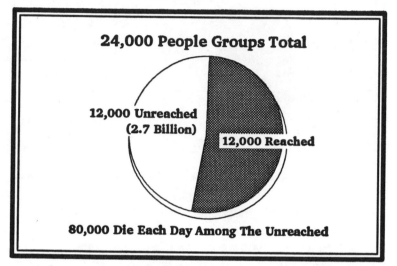

Think about it: Right now, roughly half the world's population doesn't have a chance to say "yes" or "no" to the blessing of salvation in Christ. Pray that our hearts are broken knowing that every day nearly 80,000 individuals in unreached people groups perish without God and without hope (that's 55 people a minute or roughly one person every second).

God's purpose is to see that all those 12,000 groups of people have a church. About 4,000 distinct Muslim people groups make up the largest cultural bloc of the unreached. Han Chinese people groups form another large segment of people without a viable church. Hindu, Buddhist, and tribal people groups also are major cultural blocs without a Gospel witness.

There's an easy way to remember them. Think of your thumb: T-H-U-M-B. *T* stands for Tribals, *H* is for the Hindus, *U* (turned sideways!) is for the Chinese, *M* is for the Muslims, and *B* is for the Buddhists. All are in desperate need of having someone reach out to them.

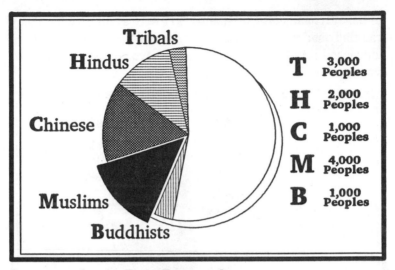

T	**3,000** Peoples
H	**2,000** Peoples
C	**1,000** Peoples
M	**4,000** Peoples
B	**1,000** Peoples

Resources for the Task: Personnel

Half the world's individuals have a church within their cultures and can learn about the Lord, and half the world does not have a church. If you were God, where would you send your best laborers, to the reached half of the world's population or to the unreached half?

It only makes sense that sending the best laborers to the unreached half is what the Lord, the Head of the Body of Christ, would do. So what is the Body doing? Look carefully through the "Great Imbalance Diagram" on the next page until it hits you: We're not doing well at all, yet.

Almost 90 percent of all our foreign missionaries go to the reached people groups, the half of the world where there already is a church established. Now, there's nothing wrong with that. Because where the church has been planted, it grows unbelievably, and these fledgling churches need encouragement and workers. Missionaries to reached fields are viable ministries.

But, we've got to face up to the fact that only 10 percent of our foreign missionary force is going to the totally unreached half of the world, where roughly one person every second dies without ever hearing about Christ.

That's foreign missionaries. If you were to look at the number of full-time Christian workers, you'd find for every worker going to unreached peoples, 171 go to a culture where there already is an established church. That's 99.9 percent.

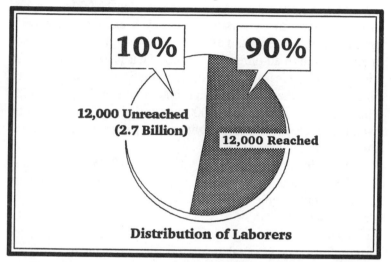

10% **90%**

12,000 Unreached (2.7 Billion)

12,000 Reached

Distribution of Laborers

Let's be blunt with ourselves: Is this imbalance of laborers God's will? Is this the way God planned it? Or is it perhaps evidence of the disobedience of the Bride of Christ in not responding to the commission God has given us to do? Are we doing what is good in light of what is best?

Resources for the Task: Finances

Gird yourself for a few more uncomfortable factors before we get to the encouraging news of what believers are doing to establish a church in every people group on the globe.

On the average, for every dollar that gets put into the offering plate in the United States, 96 cents go right back into the American Christian culture. Out of the remaining 4 cents for the Great Commission task, 3.5 cents go to the world's people groups where there's already a church. Less than one penny goes to reach the unreached peoples of the world where there is no church. This is the product of an A > B theology.

The Need for Resources

If the Body of Christ were to tackle the task of the Great

Commission in earnest, what would be needed in terms of personnel and finances? Not to mention prayer power!

Addressing the question of how many new missionaries are needed to effectively penetrate the remaining 12,000 unreached people groups, many missiologists say a team of eight well-trained missionaries could effectively be used by God to plant a viable church in an unreached group. That is, 96,000 new missionaries are necessary, since current missionaries are deployed in other areas where, again, their ministries are critical to growing churches. Adding another 4,000 new missionaries to the total would take care of the natural attrition of retirement within the evangelical missionary force.

What finances are necessary for the task? Support for these 100,000 individual missionaries and provision for their ministry projects would require, experts suggest, an additional $1.5 billion dollars annually!

That's the discouraging news of world evangelization, the discomforting news of what is happening in this world.

The Resources Available

The good news is this: We can do it. We have the resources.

Remember Deuteronomy 32, where God orders the inheritance of the nations in direct proportion to the number of the sons of Israel? God didn't allow the nations to grow any faster than He let Israel grow, because if revival ever broke out, He would be able to realistically reach every nation through His chosen people. Has He maintained that ratio today?

Believe it! For every single unreached people group in the world today, there are 416 evangelical churches. For every one of these unreached people groups, there are 41,600 evangelical believers!

God will accomplish His purpose. The gates of hell that lock in the unreached peoples of the world can't stand against His Church. At the end of time Christ will be exalted with the song "...and with your blood you purchased men for God from every tribe and language and people and nation" (Revelation 5:9). So it's only a matter of when and through whom.

Let's simply look at America. Of the 70 million Evangelicals in America, 17.5 million are aged 18-35. The 100,000 new missionaries needed are only half of 1 percent of these young people available in the United States of America alone.

American Evangelicals have $850 billion of disposable annual income. About one-fifth of 1 percent of that income, $1.5 billion, could support the needed 12,000 church-planting teams. That's one nickel of every free dollar we have.

But this isn't a job for just American believers. With 430 million other believers worldwide, obviously the resources are available. We can establish a church movement in every unreached people group, and then help those new believers to evangelize their own people group.

We can do it if we will.

The Timing Is Everything

Remember when we talked briefly about Matthew 24:14: "And this Gospel of the kingdom will be preached in the whole world as a testimony to all nations, and then the end will come"? Again, regardless of your theological position on the timing of the events of the last days, it's obvious that the accomplishment of God's unchanging purpose on earth is linked to the end.

Think through the implications of the following passages:

- Matthew 28:18-20 disciple "all nations...to the very end of the age"
- Acts 1:6-8 "witnesses...to the ends of the earth" (v.8), "restore the kingdom to Israel" (v.6)
- Romans 11:25-26 "until the full number of the Gentiles has come in and so all Israel will be saved"
- Revelation 5:9 "[The Lamb] purchased men for God from every tribe and language and people and nation" (His breaking the seals of the scroll initiating a new era).

Let's look at another interesting passage, II Peter 3:12, where we're commanded to "look forward to the day of God and speed its coming"! How can we possibly speed the coming of the day of the Lord? Perhaps by reaching all nations, tongues, tribes, and peoples so that His promise to Abraham can be fulfilled.

Humans are almost driven to insist that everything will go on as it has since the beginning of creation (II Peter 3:4), but God reminds us that there is a definite time limit for what He is doing on the earth: "until the coming of the salvation that is ready to be revealed in the last time" (I Peter 1:5). God is waiting to see the full number of all ethnic groups reached. Then He's going to come.

We can speed the day! "Selah."

Take a big look at the history of God's people and their efforts to evangelize the world. From the time of Noah to now, what have we done?

The Jews, as we've seen, faltered in their world evangelization campaign. But God worked in spite of their disobedience.

Christ's disciples seemed to catch a glimpse of vision for the peoples of the world, but it was just a small, hesitant glimpse. Many believe that the Twelve never really caught the vision at all since they determined to remain in Jerusalem. It was Paul and Barnabas who owned that vision and first went on into Gentile territory.

After that came 300 years of persecution, and that persecution spread the Gospel throughout the Mediterranean region. Then Emperor Constantine made Christianity the official religion of the Roman Empire. You would think it a good move, but it was actually a very destructive move, because now everyone could seem to have become a Christian. In fact, because everyone virtually had to be a Christian, there was no cost in following Christ. There was little emphasis on spreading this bland state religion to the ends of the earth.

During the Dark Ages, it seems that the idea of the Great Commission wasn't even considered. There were small groups of believers, of course, with small ideas of reaching the world, but a movement as a whole never came about. During this reign of barbarism, naturally, God was accomplishing His determined will to spread the good news to all peoples through a series of migrations. As people groups moved, the believers among them began to spread the blessing of redemption in Christ. Even the forays of the Vikings and other "barbarians" into Christian lands spurred on the spread of God's blessing. The misguided Crusades fueled some spread of the awareness of God's plan of redemption but again, on the whole, believers seldom united with a sense of purpose in blessing the nations to the ends of the earth.

Even the era of the Reformation produced little vision for the world. Luther's and Calvin's Protestantism explored the theological aspects of personal salvation in Christ, but seemed to remain focused on the top line. There were only a few groups (notably, the Moravians) that caught a sense of God's great global purpose. There was no sense of a movement of God's people as a whole until the 1790s. Then an Englishman by the name of William Carey announced, "You know what? I'd like to go evangelize the heathen in India." His church elders responded to him: "Young man, when God wants to reach the heathen, He'll do it without your help and without ours."

Astounded, Carey wrote a little booklet about our obligation to evangelize the heathen throughout the world, and then proceeded to practice what he preached. He headed for India and spawned a movement to evangelize the coastlands of the world's continents. The men and women of this movement were stalwart, no-holds-barred zealots who often set sail with their belongings in a casket because they knew they only had an average of two years to live in the disease-ridden areas. They felt the priority of evangelizing the world was far greater than saving their own lives. But, for various reasons, the first wave of modern mission interest began to die down.

Then in the 1860s, Hudson Taylor fostered a second movement reaching out to the unreached in the inland regions. He founded the China Inland Mission, now called Overseas Missionary Fellowship. Also during that time came Sudan Interior Mission. Out of this movement came Africa Inland Mission, Regions Beyond Missionary Union, and others. Nearly 20,000 new laborers volunteered as missionaries during these years.

Still, though championed by the amazing energy of the Student Volunteer movements in America, even this powerful second wave of reaching the unreached began to fizzle in the mid-twentieth century.

Women played a key role in both movements. Ruth Tucker and Walter Liefeld in Daughters of the Church felt the women's role was the backbone of it all.

But we now find ourselves in the possibility of a third movement, a third wave or era in modern missions. Perhaps the final era.

Responding to the calls of Cameron Townsend and Donald McGavran in the second half of this century to go to the culturally isolated "hidden" or "unreached" peoples, many believers sense that this third wave is surging to the breaking point in this last decade before the year 2000. God is doing amazing things in our world. He's sending Navajo missionaries to the Mongolians, shaking up American finances for His worldwide cause, blasting open the Iron Curtain, raising a movement of excited disciples ready to go anywhere and do anything. He's harvesting more than 70,000 new believers every day. Eminent world watchers sense an upcoming burst of God's power in this final decade of the twentieth century, during these closing years of the second millennium.

Yet in light of the 4,000 or so years man has been here since the time of Noah, notice that in the past 200 years God has poured out his Spirit in a new and unparalleled way. Why only now?

Opportunity for Harvest

The population growth of Planet Earth is skyrocketing as never before. Billions of people have lived on this planet throughout all of recorded history.

To have the first one billion people alive at the same time took 9,830 years. To bring the population to two billion took an additional 100 years. To bring the population to three billion took an additional 30 years. To bring it to four billion took an additional 15 years, and to five billion took another 14 years. The next one billion will take 11 years.

What took 9,830 years to do the first time is now going to take only 11 years to do!

The population of this planet is exploding in exponential growth. By the year 2000, world population will reach about 6.26 billion. Often, that population growth is seen as a cause for discouragement in reaching the world's unreached. Actually, it's an incredible time of opportunity for completing the Great Commission! If there was ever a time to be alive on this planet called Earth, it is today.

Since population growth is no surprise to God in His unchanging purpose, perhaps we simply need to sit down and realize that if we reached the world now, we'd be able to make an impact on more people than has ever before been possible.

These are exciting days as God is pouring out His Spirit and giving us fresh insights into His purpose for the world's peoples. Why us? Why now?

First, because He is aware, in advance, of our future obedience. But second, the movement to reach every people with the Gospel is growing because now, more than at any other time in history, there are simply more people to bring into the Kingdom in a brief period of time!

God has entrusted us with the technology, the transportation, the communications, the finances, and the power to finish the Great Commission. God has provided everything so that we can accomplish His task in a more concentrated time frame than was ever previously possible. For example, it is now possible to codify whole languages into computerized translation programs to produce Bible translations and church-planting tools in a fraction of the time it required just 20 years ago. You can be anywhere on the globe in 24 hours. We've got the tools. We can do it. We can evangelize the world.

We are living in the most exciting time in the history of the world, the unfolding of God's unchanging purpose. The largest Christian denominations have dedicated this decade to world outreach. Many Christian leaders believe these final years of the twentieth century will witness the greatest spiritual harvest the world has ever seen.

Believers in various countries are "adopting" unreached

peoples to target. For example, South American Christians are planning to send teams to 3,000 unreached groups. North American churches are targeting 6,000.

Christians worldwide are getting excited, realistic, and specific about throwing themselves into the final era of God's unchanging purpose. And prayers are being lifted up beseeching God that *you* be a part of the plan. "Selah."

For Further Thought

For individual or group study:

- List other ideas new to you from this chapter's discussion.
- List questions raised in this segment of study.
- Scan the chapter, noting especially meaningful references and marking these in your Bible.
- In a brief summary, write down the basic information in this chapter; then explain that information to at least two other believers this week.
- Glance back over previous chapters to be reminded of the various people groups you've met in this study. Then get serious about praying for them for at least 15 minutes this week.
- Pray that churches around the world would begin to think about adopting an unreached people group.

11—An Attainable Goal

It's a fact: If the Body of Christ began to think strategically and would target resources to send one team to plant one church to each unreached people group, we could evangelize the world in our generation. Easily.

But of course the big word is *if*—if the Body of Christ begins to think strategically, if it responds to the unchanging nature of God's purpose. Frankly, it seems that many people in the Body of Christ are not thinking strategically. They act as if they have no clue what God is doing, and as if He has not made clear His unchanging purpose from Genesis to Revelation to reach every people group in the world.

The consequences of this unclear vision of God's purpose are obvious. King Solomon stated that "where there is no vision, the people perish" or, more literally, "lose restraint" (Proverbs 29:18 KJV). People naturally lose focus and have no reason to discipline themselves, even in moral areas, if there is no constraining task to tackle.

If the Great Commission were a mandate to reach 5 billion individual people with the Gospel, it would be obvious that God gave us not the Great Commission, but Mission Impossible.

Without a very clear, realistic vision, it's easy to think, "Lord, I haven't even reached my next-door neighbor yet. How could I ever reach more than 2 billion people? Lord, I think I'll just stay here and try to be a good Christian."

But when you realize God has commanded us to reach 12,000 distinct ethnic groups, all of a sudden the job is achievable. Perhaps you decide: Actually, my church could adopt one of those groups, and, especially if we got together with nine other churches in our town, surely we could see a church movement planted in that group. Then those new believers could reach out to their own culture in more effective ways than a foreign missionary ever could.

The Great Commission is very, very attainable. It is within our reach if we begin to pray that God would open up the eyes of the Church and allow us to think strategically about world evangelization.

Look What God is Doing!

If you're in a dull little corner of Christendom, it is critical that you realize what God is doing these days around the globe. Here are a few highlights.

- 1,600 new churches are opening every week worldwide!
- 28,000 become believers each day in China. Conservative estimates say there are 40-50 million Christians in that country.
- 20,000 become believers every day in Africa. That continent was 3 percent Christian in 1900 and is over 40 percent Christian today.
- A total of 70,000 become Christians every day!
- In 1900, Korea had no Protestant church; it was deemed impossible to penetrate. Today, Korea is 30 percent Christian, with 4,000 churches in Seoul alone.
- In Indonesia, the percentage of Christians is so high the government won't print the statistic—which is probably nearing 25 percent of the population.
- After 70 years of oppression in the now defunct Soviet Union, Christians recently numbered about 100 million—5 times the number in the Communist Party and 36 percent of the population.
- God is creatively sending Chinese believers to reach Tibetans, Hondurans to reach Laplanders and Mongolians.
- Where the Church has been planted, it's growing like wildfire. The good news is breaking loose worldwide.
- More Muslims in Iran have come to Christ since 1980 than in the previous 1,000 years combined.
- In AD 100, there were 360 non-Christians per true believer. Today the ratio is seven to every believer.

- In AD 100 there were twelve unreached people groups per congregation of believers. Today there are 416 congregations for every unreached people group.

That's what God is doing. What are we doing now to ride the crest of this wave?

That unchanging purpose places a greater priority on the mandate of the covenant than on our own personal goals, dreams, desires and security. Remember Naaman's little Hebrew slave girl? She had goals. She had things she wanted to accomplish, but God allowed her to become a slave to a foreigner because of His love, His intense love for a Gentile (II Kings 5:1-27).

Jonah had plans. He had legitimate fears. But God had a job beyond Jonah's plans and fears. It's as if God said, "I've got something better for you, Jonah. I want you to go to Nineveh, because I love the Ninevites" (Jonah 1-4).

God is willing to forfeit our ease to see His goals and purposes brought about. That's what the Lordship of Jesus Christ is all about. Jesus says in Luke 14:33 that we must be willing to give up ownership of all we possess if we are to be His disciples. The possessions aren't just material things. We possess goals, dreams, desires, careers, all sorts of intangible things. And we must be willing to lay these at the foot of the Cross if we want to see Him accomplish through us all that we can do, and even more than we can do.

Your Part in The Big Picture

Perhaps you're a young person striking out on a career. Or you're older, struggling with the quandaries of a career change. The questions are familiar to all of us. Some might ask, "God, what are You calling me to be? Do You want me to be a Christian housewife, and really do a good job at that?" Others might say, "Lord, am I to be intensively involved in discipleship and prayer? Is that where You want me?" Still others, "Lord, is my domain, my reservoir of life-giving water, supposed to be that of a Christian engineer? Am I simply to be a testimony to those at my office? I'd like to be a good Christian chemist. Or how about a lawyer? Maybe I'll teach Sunday School on the side for a ministry. Maybe I'll be a carpenter, or a pastor, or a real estate agent. Lord, what do You want me to do?"

Somehow, we begin to get a bit self-centered about God's will for our lives. The prime question seems to be: "What is God's will for my life?" as if A were far greater than B! Might it be a Christian dentist, might it be a children's worker? Am I to do this or to do that? And we think that each possibility is basically unrelated to all the other roles of God's people. We think of our career as an isolated little lake way over here and God's will for another believer's career as a little lake way over there.

But we must begin to think of ourselves, not as isolated pools, but as contributing parts of the whole composite of God's will. Each of our lives can release its potential into the mighty river of God's ultimate plan to reach all nations.

If you are a Christian pastor, you're to be equipping men and women to have a vision for the glory of God, to disciple others to get involved in the story of the Bible of reaching all the nations. If you are a Christian mother or father, you're to train and raise up godly children who will be so sharp and so well versed in His word that they can intercede for missions and even go cross-culturally to reach the nations.

If you are a chemist or a doctor or a lawyer, you're being blessed by God with financial blessings, among others, so that you can turn around and be a blessing to those who are more directly involved in reaching the nations. And you, yourself, can be involved in reaching the nations through prayer and through encouragement of other workers who go to the nations...even through reaching internationals in your area.

But you're not simply to be a dentist or real estate agent or salesman off by yourself. You're to plug into God's big-picture plan to reach all the nations. Everything we do is to reach that zenith of seeing every people group reached and thus bring a greater amount of glory to God.

If you have a vision to reach your neighborhood, your town, or even all of America, rejoice! You're seeing God's heart for five percent of the world's population. But reach your Jerusalem and Judea, clothe the needy and feed the hungry, witness across the street, and stand up for the unborn with an expanded vision of God's whole heart for the uttermost parts of the world, and get to know the rest of your God!

Minister within your own people group to bring your neighbors to Christ; equip them to join the cause of reaching every people group with the Gospel. Encourage the growing churches on established mission fields by training them to be sending churches. Directly or indirectly, be a part of God's historic purpose to add to the Body of Christ those "purchased with His blood from every tribe and tongue and people and nation."

God has a job for you, and it has to do with the 12,000 unreached people groups of this planet. It is God's ultimate purpose for today's busy Christian.

The Countdown!

We're almost 4,000 years into God's promise to Abraham that all the people groups would be blessed with redemption, and the plan is intensifying. Hundreds of mission groups worldwide have seen AD 2000 as an arbitrary target date to finish the task of reaching each people group.

Since, as we've studied, Jesus simply said, "This Gospel of the Kingdom shall be preached in the whole world for a testimony unto all nations; and then shall the end come" (Matthew 24:14), you might feel uncomfortable about AD 2000 as a target date to see mission teams among each of the 12,000 unreached groups...as if the year 2000 is then some prediction of the return of Christ. Relax. The countdown of people groups to be reached by the year 2000 is simply an arresting way to suggest that we can complete the Great Commission within a few years if we will. At a world-level conference in Edinburgh, Scotland, 70 mission groups from 37 countries adopted the phrase "A Church for Every People By the Year 2000."

But if date-setting feels awkward, imagine that it's 2041 and we can reach all remaining groups within seven years. Would 2048 be a less threatening target date than 2000?

But why wait, when every day 80,000 unreached souls go to

hell—one every time your heart beats (which is one of those uncomfortable Bible truths we don't like to think about)? If the lost weren't lost, why would God command us to disciple the nations at all? The Bible says these very real people, individual by individual, are without God and without hope (Ephesians 2:12). Study this distressing fact in the Word. Then ask yourself, "Why wait?"

We can establish a church for every people group in the next few years. And you can be a part of this urgent, historic, big-picture priority.

Your Part in the Big Picture

It is time to pray and beseech God to raise up laborers to go to the very ends of the earth. The verb Jesus used to "thrust laborers out" means to actually push them out, even if it's against their own will. It's the same Greek verb, *ekballo,* used when Jesus cast the money changers out of the temple or when you cast a demon out of a person. Why such prayers? Probably because God knew how infatuated we would be with the top line. It is time that we do the job that will be the finale of 4,000 years.

Let's get radical and simply obey the Great Commission to reach every people group in the world. Now. Let's pray for it. Fast for it. Encourage our brothers and sisters to put their lives on the line. We have an unparalleled opportunity—a window that, for the moment, is wide open.

Many people are saying that in the year 2000 we should present Jesus a birthday gift—the gift of an evangelized world. That's why many young people are giving up top-line-focused careers. Retired couples are giving up "the good life" and joining teams overseas. Thousands of young and older believers are giving up the BMW's and the pursuit of the big bucks, and instead are saying, "Lord, I want to be used strategically by You to see this world evangelized."

The Catch

If the Biblical mandate is so clear, if the big picture of what God is doing in our world is so exciting, if the 12,000 remaining groups can be reached within several years, if millions are dying without God and without hope, why isn't all Christendom buzzing with the news that we can finish the task?

Because there's a catch. There's a cost involved.

Obedience costs. Real discipleship costs. The price is giving up any small, local agendas that detract from God's global cause. The cost is forsaking our little lives, giving up claims of ownership and security. The requirement for ministries is to cooperate selflessly rather than needlessly duplicating efforts and competing for funds.

Obedience means shifting our focus to being a blessing instead of just being blessed—the vision problem Haggai pinpointed as the downfall of Israel.

The price of being a part of God's global purpose is losing your life for His sake.

Active participation in the big picture of God's plan is also dangerous. It's the danger of signing on in wartime as a soldier who doesn't entangle himself in the affairs of everyday life (II Timothy 2:4). Battling the powers and world forces (Ephesians 6:12) that have bound these 12,000 groups for thousands of years means spiritual warfare; and warfare means casualties, body counts, blood, sweat, and tears.

God's big purpose on this planet is not a game. It's not a health spa regimen. It's war. And war is never nice.

Maybe too many Christians have been led to believe that the true believer's life is supposed to be nice, respectable, predictable, and smooth. Or maybe they actually have counted the cost of discipleship in God's big plan and have decided they're too weak for real battle and refuse to trust the Commander's strength.

But what about you? Is there any good reason you and your fellowship aren't taking seriously the mandate in God's historic purpose to disciple the nations? You could "adopt" a people group and see to it that the countdown number is lowered to 11,999!

For Further Thought

For group or individual study:

- Explain how attainable the Great Commission really is.
- List the five unreached blocks of mankind.
- Share some of these simple statistics with a friend.
- Read through the appendices.
- Explain the basics of Islam in your Sunday School class.
- Seek to find Muslims in your area and befriend them. Ask them to share with you what Islam means to them.
- Choose five application steps from Appendix B and act on them.

Islam: A Neglected Challenge

Consider one very significant category of unreached people groups—the Muslims of the world.

Few American Christians know much about Islam. This ignorance keeps them from acting or having a significant role in seeing that churches become a reality in the heart of the Muslim world. God cannot lead where there is no knowledge. So open yourself a bit more to His leading and learn about Islam.

The word *Islam,* in its purest essence, means "submission to God." A Muslim (one who follows Islam) is "one who submits to God." The very heart of the religion is that Muslims are trying to seek the face of God.

Today they represent 17 percent of the world's population, nearly one out of every five people on the face of the earth. They span the globe, but reside mainly in the Asian area. Only one-quarter of the Muslim world is Arabic-speaking.

There are 44 predominantly Muslim countries throughout the world. In these countries either there has never been a church established, the church is too small and inward to influence Muslims, or it has become extinct.

Some churches in these countries are basically indifferent to their Islamic neighbors' needs for Christ. One pastor in a predominantly Muslim country said, "Hell...It's the best place for them." There are such radical differences between Muslims and Christians that most "historical Christians" in this man's area would prefer to see Muslims go to hell. Churches in largely Islamic countries are generally constituted almost entirely of people from non-Muslim backgrounds, with cultural patterns abhorrent to Muslims.

Though these statistics are alarming, the news gets even

worse. Less than two percent of our total Protestant missionary force works among Muslims. This means that there are more missionaries to the state of Alaska than there are to the entire Muslim world. We simply have not made reaching Muslims a priority. Our financial patterns are revealing: Less than one-tenth of every penny of every dollar given to the local church in North America goes to the Muslim world.

What Muslims Believe

Muslims believe they must do five simple things to work their way to heaven.

First is their witness. They must confess that there is no god but Allah, and that Muhammed is his prophet.

Second, a Muslim must pray five times a day. These prayers are short, lasting an average of two minutes, and are said from memory. Muslims pray at approximately an hour before sunrise, 10:00 a.m., 1:00 p.m., 4:00 p.m., and about an hour after sunset.

Third, a Muslim needs to tithe his income. Muslims tithe two percent of their income to help the poor. Many Muslims give their tithe directly to needy people on the street.

The fast of Ramadan is the fourth way to earn entrance into heaven. The Muslim fast is different from the Christian fast in that it lasts for one lunar month from sunrise to sunset. During this time of day, Muslims are not allowed to have anything pass down their throats. This way they relate to the hungry of the world.

Fifth, a journey to Mecca (the birthplace of Islam) must be undertaken if one can afford it. This is a very holy pilgrimage for the Muslims, and they derive great satisfaction from it.

Some missiologists add a sixth requirement, the *jihad,* which literally means "exerting force for God." One's *jihad* might be accomplished through writing a book about Islam, trying to share one's faith with someone, or physically fighting for the cause of Islam. This is what Iranian leader Khomeini sustained for so many years against Iraq: a holy fight, a *jihad* for the cause of Islam.

In Islam, the only eternal security one has is dying in *jihad.*

If death comes during *jihad,* one is guaranteed the keys to heaven. (Now you can understand why there are individuals driving a truckload of dynamite into U.S. Marine barracks, killing themselves and the Marines. In doing so, they guaranteed their entrance into heaven.)

In essence, Muslims will tell you that they have a good angel on one shoulder and a bad angel on the other. When you get to heaven, there will be a judgment day, and if your good works outweigh the bad works, you will probably go to a sort of purgatory and eventually make it to heaven. If the reverse is true, you will go to hell forever.

Some Islamic beliefs are similar to Christian beliefs. Muslims believe in one God, as well as good and bad angels. They also believe in many prophets. All Muslims believe in Adam and Eve, Moses, David, Abraham, and even Jesus, but their final prophet is Muhammed, who gave the ultimate revelation about Islam.

They believe in certain holy books: the Torah (the first five books of the Old Testament), the Zabur (the Psalms), the Ingil (the New Testament, officially only the four Gospels), and their Koran.

The Koran is considered to summarize all the other books while adding more truth. (Think of it as the "Reader's Digest condensed version" of all of the other books.) Muslims believe that our Bible has been corrupted and cannot be trusted; thus they have no copies of it and do not feel that they need it, because "the Koran covers it all" and needs nothing added to it.

A Place to Belong

In reality, what keeps a Muslim a Muslim is 90 percent cultural and only 10 percent theological.

Muslims need to belong to an extended group of individuals in order to feel secure. They do not buy the Western idea of "Be independent; be Number One." Usually, the primary group to which they belong is their extended family. It is in that extended family that they find security and meaning and purpose. In Muslim terminology, this belonging is *ummah*

Picture it. A missionary sits down and gives a Muslim the invitation to come to Christ. What is going through the Muslim's mind?

"You mean you want me to leave my extended family where all my social, financial, and physical security are? You say that all of that is wrong and my family and friends are going to hell?...Sure, tell me another one!"

Leaving his *ummah* is the hardest thing a Muslim faces. The theological differences between Christianity and Islam are tough, but Muslims can get over them. Theology is only 10 percent of the problem.

Complicating the issue even more is how Muslims view Christianity. Muslims believe that we worship three Gods: God the father, God the son, and God the mother, and that that threesome came to be when God came down to earth, saw Mary, lusted after her, and had sex with her. (No wonder they believe Christianity is simply "out to lunch.")

This concept of an immoral religion is confirmed in Muslims' minds when they turn on the television and watch "Christian" programs. They assume that "Dallas" and "Dynasty" are Christian TV programs and that they exemplify Christianity.

The overall effect? In considering the claims of Christ, most Muslims start at a negative 15 rather than 0. They need to work their way out of these misconceptions before they can hear the Good News of Christ.

Frontiers:
A Challenge to Respond

Does the challenge of reaching Muslims sound disheartening, or simply challenging? There are those Christians who are excited about reaching Muslims for Christ, who believe that God is initiating a great work in the Islamic world. One such group of people is Frontiers.

Frontiers is looking to place 2,000 new missionaries on 200 new teams in the Islamic world by the year 2000. It is our goal to send teams to see churches become a reality.

Frontiers has five distinctives.

First, we work solely with Muslims. We do not work with Hindus, Buddhists, Chinese, or tribal groups. We are a bit like Kentucky Fried Chicken: We do one thing, and try to do it right!

Second, we send out teams as opposed to individuals, for we believe that the Bible encourages this model. (For more information on how our teams work, write to Frontiers, 325 N. Stapley Dr., Mesa, Arizona 85203 and ask for our brochures titled "Questions and Answers to Frontiers" and "One in a Million.")

Third, each team goes to plant a church. We are not there only to do evangelism or discipleship; the end goal is an established church.

Fourth, we coach the teams on the field. Experienced missionaries travel frequently to visit the teams, passing along strategies and news of other teams, and helping team members catch a better understanding of what is going on in the world.

Fifth, we encourage diverse and creative approaches in pursuit of our unifying goal of seeing churches planted in the Muslim world. We realize that everyone will not fit the same mold, so we allow a wide variety of molds within Frontiers

We do not require seminary or Bible school diplomas from our candidates. A much more pressing concern is that they have a working knowledge of the Scriptures and a vital, vibrant walk with God. Each team member must also be sent out by a home church.

We accept retired couples as missionaries. We are actively recruiting individuals to "retire" on the field with our teams. Often we find these older folks to be the "glue" which holds our teams together. They make excellent witnesses since Muslims highly respect those of an older generation.

Every team is flexible. Each makes many of its own policy decisions about furlough, children's education, retirement, and finances. Team leaders decide where their team goes, and only they can approve or deny placement on their team.

As of the publication of this book, Frontiers has 65 teams either on the field or preparing to go, with over 270 missionaries on Muslim soil. We have grown very quickly in a short amount of time, and we feel that is God's stamp of approval on us.

As you continue to grow in your world vision, we would make one request—please consider the Muslims. With only one missionary for every one million Muslims, we need people like you.

You may be saying to yourself, "Hey, wait a minute, you don't even know me." You're right. But we do know the God that lives inside you....

If you are interested, please fill out the "I'm Interested" form (Appendix A) or write to: Frontiers, 325 N. Stapley Dr., Mesa, Arizona 85203, 602/834-1500.

Overview of Appendices

Appendix A

> If God has been tugging on your heart to get involved in the Muslim world, consider joining Frontiers. Your first step? Fill out the "I'm Interested" form. There is no obligation—you are merely "testing the waters." We'd love to hear from you. Or call us at 1-800-GO2-THEM (1-800-462-8436).

Appendix B

> This appendix has a listing of all the Scriptures I've found on God's dealing with the nations—the bottom line. Highlight these verses in your Bible and see how they relate to the big picture. Feel free to copy this section and pass it on.

Appendix C

> This appendix will give you 59 creative ways to implement your bottom-line vision. These are not to be legalistic or to substitute projects for long-term commitments.

Appendix D

> No church lives out a perfect $A = B$ commitment. Few live out an $A > B$ commitment to its extreme. In this appendix, you'll see two churches (both hypothetical) compared in their commitment to world evangelization. Do any characteristics match your church?

Appendix E

> This appendix shows creative ways to teach children a bottom-line vision through new verses to familiar songs.

Appendix F

> Don't finish this book until you have seen what other materials are available for you, your church, your Sunday school, and your home Bible study group.

Appendix A

"I'm Interested" . . . in possible service with Frontiers either at home or abroad.

(Use separate sheets of paper to fill out.)

Name _____Date _____
Address _____
City _____ St_____ Zip_____
Phone _____ Birthdate _____ S.S# _____
(Current address valid until: _____)
Permanent Address _____
City _____ St_____ Zip_____
Permanent Phone _____
Citizenship _____
Marital Status: Single____ Engaged____ Married____
(Wedding date: _____)
Separated____ Divorced____ Widowed____ Remarried_____
(Date: _____)
Spouse's name _____ Years Married_____
Children's name(s) and birthdates(s) and S.S.#'s

_____
_____

TELL US ABOUT YOURSELF (On another sheet)

1. Describe how and when you became a Christian.
2. Trace significant areas of your Christian growth.
3. In what ways and with what success have you helped to bring others to Christ? What further experience have you had discipling new believers?
4. Have you had any significant contact with representatives of Frontiers (especially Team Leaders or Team Coordinators)? If so, explain.
5. Give information on schools you have attended beyond high school, including college, Bible school, seminary, or other special schools. If currently in school, when do you expect to graduate?

Give information on your current and past employment record: _____

_____
_____

Every Frontiers missionary must have a sending church.
Which church will be sending you?
Church Name: _____
Denomination: _____
Address:_____
Pastor: _____
Phone: _____
Elder: _____
Phone: _____
Mission Chairman: _____
Phone: _____

How long have you taken an active role in this church? _____
Give examples of current involvement: _____
To what degree do you think the church may be providing
your finances? _____
6. Your interest in Frontiers: (use separate sheet)
• The goal of all we do is to establish indigenous churches.
  What can you envision doing to establish churches among
  Muslims, in terms of both tentmaking and actual
  church-planting?
• Frontiers believes strongly in working in teams. Describe
  any previous experiences of working on a team. What
  roles have you tended to take in group efforts?
• Describe any hesitancies you have about an overseas
  ministry as a "tentmaker"—holding a secular job in order
  to maintain residence while conducting a ministry of
  evangelism, disciple-making, and church-planting as your
  main goals.
• Describe any hesitancies you have regarding support
  raising.

What is your interest?

☐ Summer / Short-term project
☐ 6 months to 1 year assignment
☐ 2 (or more) year commitment

- What might affect your availability? For example: family, romance, debt, health, other obligations.
- Do you have any questions regarding Frontiers?

Send to: Personnel Director, Frontiers, 325 N. Stapley Dr., Mesa, Arizona 85203, 602/834-1500.

Appendix B

Bottom-Line Scriptures

Gen 3: 15	Lev 18: 26-28	Jos 6: 17,25,27
Gen 12: 1-3	Lev 19: 9,10,33,34	Jos 7: 9
Gen 12: 10-20	Lev 20: 2,3	Jos 8: 33,35
Gen 13: 7	Lev 22: 17,18	Jos 9: 1-27
Gen 14: 13,18-24	Lev 23: 22	Jos 11: 1-3
Gen 15: 1-21	Lev 24: 16,22	Jos 13: 13
Gen 17: 12,13	Lev 25: 23	Jos 15: 63
Gen 17: 15,16,27	Lev 26: 45	Jos 16: 10
Gen 18: 1-33	Num 9: 14	Jos 17: 12,13
Gen 20: 2-18	Num 10: 29-32	Jos 20: 9
Gen 21: 22,23,25	Num 12: 1,2	Jud 1: 16,21,28-36
Gen 22: 1-18	Num 14: 13-19	Jud 2: 23-3: 5
Gen 23: 3-20	Num 15: 14-16,26	Jud 3: 13,14
Gen 24: 12-14,26,27	Num 19: 10	Jud 5: 24-27
Gen 24: 34-54	Num 22: 1-24: 25	Rut 1: 1-4: 22
Gen 26: 2-31	Num 32: 3,4	1Sa 4: 6-9
Gen 28: 13-15	Num 35: 15	1Sa 5: 1-6: 16
Gen 30: 27	Deu 1: 4	1Sa 9: 3,6
Gen 34: 1-31	Deu 2: 24-3: 11	1Sa 12: 22
Gen 35: 5,11,12	Deu 4: 6,25-27	1Sa 17: 1-59
Gen 37: 5-30,36	Deu 5: 6-21,32,33	1Sa 19: 8
Gen 39: 1-47: 31	Deu 7: 6-9,14	1Sa 22: 3,4
Exo 2: 24	Deu 9: 25-29	1Sa 26: 6
Exo 3: 6,8,15-22	Deu 10: 14,18,19	2Sa 7: 22-26
Exo 4: 1-17,22	Deu 11: 25	2Sa 8: 1-14
Exo 5: 1-3,24	Deu 14: 29	2Sa 10: 1-9
Exo 6: 2-8	Deu 16: 14	2Sa 11: 6-11
Exo 7: 1-11: 10	Deu 23: 7,8	2Sa 12: 29-31
Exo 14: 4-31	Deu 24: 17-22	2Sa 15: 18-22
Exo 15: 14-16,27	Deu 26: 11-13	2Sa 21: 1-9
Exo 17: 8-15	Deu 27: 19	2Sa 22: 44-46,50
Exo 18: 1,8-12	Deu 28: 10,11,64	2Sa 24: 16,18-25
Exo 19: 5,6	Deu 29: 11,22,24-29	1Ki 3: 1-4,11
Exo 22: 21	Deu 30: 1	1Ki 4: 20,21,29-34
Exo 23: 9	Deu 31: 12,16-18	1Ki 5: 1-12
Exo 23: 9,12	Deu 32: 7	1Ki 8: 16,18,19,29
Exo 32: 9-13	Jos 2: 1-24	1Ki 8: 41-43,59-61
Exo 33: 1-3,16	Jos 3: 13-17	1Ki 9: 8,9
Lev 16: 29,30	Jos 4: 19-24	1Ki 10: 1-13,23-25
Lev 17: 8-10,13,15	Jos 5: 1,14	1Ki 11: 1-13

1Ki 14: 21-24,31
1Ki 17: 7-18: 45
1Ki 19: 15
1Ki 20: 1-34
2Ki 1: 2
2Ki 3: 1-27
2Ki 4: 8-37
2Ki 4: 42-44
2Ki 5: 1-20
2Ki 6: 8-23
2Ki 8: 1,2
2Ki 13: 20,21
2Ki 15: 29,30
2Ki 16: 9-12
2Ki 17: 1-6,23-41
2Ki 18: 10-12,17-37
2Ki 19: 10-19,35,36
2Ki 24: 10-17
1Ch 2: 4
1Ch 5: 23-26
1Ch 11: 11,12,27-47
1Ch 14: 17
1Ch 16: 8,14-18
1Ch 16: 23-31
1Ch 17: 20-24
1Ch 21: 15
1Ch 22: 7
2Ch 2: 1-12,17,18
2Ch 6: 13,32,33
2Ch 8:7,8
2Ch 9: 1-9,22-24
2Ch 14: 9-15
2Ch 17: 10,11
2Ch 10: 1-30
2Ch 26: 8
2Ch 27: 9,22,23
2Ch 30: 25
2Ch 32: 9-23,31
2Ch 36: 13,25
Ezr 1: 1-7: 28
Neh 1: 8-6: 15
Neh 9: 2,10
Neh 10: 31
Neh 13: 16-18
Est 1: 1-10: 3
Psa 2: 7-12
Psa 7: 6-8
Psa 8: 1-9

Psa 9: 7-12,15-20
Psa 18: 49,50
Psa 23: 27-31
Psa 24: 1-7
Psa 25: 11
Psa 33: 8-14
Psa 36: 7
Psa 40: 2,3,16
Psa 44: 11,14
Psa 45: 17
Psa 46: 10
Psa 47: 1-4,7-9
Psa 48: 2,10
Psa 49: 1-20
Psa 50: 1
Psa 57: 5,9-11
Psa 58: 10,11
Psa 59: 13
Psa 64: 9,10
Psa 65: 5-8
Psa 66: 1-20
Psa 67: 1-7
Psa 68: 29-35
Psa 69: 34-36
Psa 72: 11-15
Psa 72: 17-19
Psa 76: 11,12
Psa 77: 14
Psa 79: 9,10
Psa 82: 8
Psa 83: 13-18
Psa 86: 9,17
Psa 87: 4-6
Psa 94: 6,7
Psa 96: 1-13
Psa 97: 1-9
Psa 98: 1-9
Psa 99: 1-5
Psa 100: 1-5
Psa 102: 12-22
Psa 105: 1-4
Psa 106: 8
Psa 108: 1-9
Psa 113: 1-9
Psa 114: 7,8
Psa 117: 1,2
Psa 126: 1-3
Psa 137: 4-6

Psa 145: 9-13,21
Psa 146: 5-10
Psa 148: 7-14
Psa 150: 6
Ecl 3: 11,14
Ecl 5: 1-7
Ecl 7: 13,14,20
Ecl 8: 13
Ecl 11: 05
Ecl 12: 13,14
Isa 2: 2-4,19
Isa 6: 1-13
Isa 7: 18-25
Isa 8: 17
Isa 9: 1,2
Isa 10: 20-23
Isa 11: 9-12
Isa 13: 2-5
Isa 14: 1
Isa 16: 1-5,11-13
Isa 17: 3
Isa 17: 6-8
Isa 18: 2-7
Isa 19: 1-25
Isa 21: 9,10
Isa 23: 6-9,17,18
Isa 24: 13-16
Isa 25: 1-8
Isa 26: 9,11,18
Isa 27: 5,6
Isa 29: 9-12,18
Isa 30: 20-22
Isa 35: 1-10
Isa 37: 20
Isa 40: 3-5
Isa 41: 1,17-42: 21
Isa 45: 5-7,15,16
Isa 45: 21-24
Isa 48: 6-11,18,19
Isa 49: 3,6,7
Isa 49: 22,23,26
Isa 51: 1-6
Isa 52: 9,10,13-15
Isa 55: 3-5,8-13
Isa 56: 1-8
Isa 59: 19
Isa 60: 1-1-16
Isa 61: 1-6,9-11

Isa 62: 1-6,10-12
Isa 63: 11-14,17
Isa 64: 7
Isa 65: 1,8,9-12
Isa 66: 8,15-21
Jer 1: 4-10
Jer 2: 3
Jer 3: 17
Jer 4: 1,2,15-17
Jer 6: 18-20
Jer 7: 6
Jer 9: 25,26
Jer 10: 6,7
Jer 10: 10-16,25
Jer 12: 14-16
Jer 13: 1-11
Jer 14: 7
Jer 15: 02
Jer 16: 19-21
Jer 18: 1-10
Jer 22: 3,8,9
Jer 25: 8-38
Jer 26: 6
Jer 27: 1-11
Jer 29: 14-18
Jer 31: 3-14
Jer 32: 19-23,27
Jer 33: 5-13
Jer 40: 1-5
Jer 44: 30
Jer 49: 7-22
Jer 50: 1-7,46
Jer 51: 1-58
Lam 1: 18,19,21
Eze 3: 5-7
Eze 5: 5-8,14,15
Eze 6: 8-10,13,14
Eze 11: 16
Eze 12: 2,15,16
Eze 14: 7,8,21-23
Eze 16: 1-14,27
Eze 16: 35-42,59-63
Eze 17: 1-24
Eze 19: 4,8,9
Eze 20: 8-14,22-26
Eze 20: 44,48
Eze 21: 2-5
Eze 22: 4-6

Eze 22: 14-16,29
Eze 23: 1-48
Eze 24: 25-27
Eze 25: 1-26: 6
Eze 28: 20-29: 9
Eze 29: 12-16
Eze 30: 1-26
Eze 32: 9-15
Eze 33: 29
Eze 34: 27,30
Eze 35: 3-15
Eze 36: 16-36
Eze 37: 13,14
Eze 37: 23-28
Eze 38: 14-23
Eze 39: 1-8,21-24
Eze 39: 27-29
Eze 44: 9
Eze 47: 22,23
Dan 1: 1-6; 28
Dan 9: 15,18,19
Hos 4: 6,7
Hos 7: 11-16
Hos 8: 8-10
Hos 10: 10
Hos 11: 5,6,8-11
Hos 14: 4-8
Joe 2: 17-20,30-32
Joe 3: 1-17
Amo 1: 3-15
Amo 2: 1-5,9-11
Amo 4: 10
Amo 9: 7,9,11,12
Oba 1: 1-4,15,16
Jon 1: 1-4: 10
Mic 1: 2-2: 13
Mic 4: 2,3,10-15
Mic 5: 4,5,8,9,15
Mic 6: 9-16
Mic 7: 10-17
Nah 1: 1-3: 19
Hab 2: 14
Zep 2: 11
Zep 3: 8-20
Hag 2: 7,8,20-23
Zec 1: 10-21
Zec 2: 10-13
Zec 4: 8-14

Zec 6: 1-8
Zec 7: 10,13,14
Zec 8: 9-13,20-23
Zec 9: 4-7,10
Zec 10: 9-12
Zec 12: 1-9
Zec 13: 1-9
Zec 14: 1-9,16-21
Mal 1: 4,5,10,11,14
Mal 3: 16
Mat 1: 3,5,6
Mat 3: 1-12
Mat 4: 12-25
Mat 4: 12-25
Mat 5: 1-7: 28
Mat 8: 5-12
Mat 9: 26,31,35-38
Mat 10: 18
Mat 12: 15-21,38-42
Mat 13: 11-23,31-50
Mat 15: 1-39
Mat 16: 13-19
Mat 18: 1-19: 1
Mat 21: 12,13,33-44
Mat 22: 2-10
Mat 24: 3-14,27-31
Mat 25: 31-46
Mat 26: 10-13
Mat 28: 18-20
Mar 1: 2-9,14,15
Mar 1: 23-28,38,39
Mar 2: 15-17
Mar 3: 7-12
Mar 5: 18-20
Mar 6: 14
Mar 7: 14-30
Mar 8: 1-10,34-38
Mar 9: 1
Mar 11: 11-18
Mar 12: 1-12
Mar 13: 10,27
Mar 14: 3-9
Mar 15: 21
Mar 16: 14-20
Luk 3: 3-6
Luk 4: 14-19,23-27
Luk 5: 15
Luk 6: 17-19

Luk 7: 1-10,17
Luk 8: 4-8,22-39
Luk 9: 46-56
Luk 10: 1-37
Luk 11: 18-32
Luk 13: 6-9
Luk 14: 15-24
Luk 15: 1-32
Luk 17: 11-19
Luk 19: 11-27,45,46
Luk 20: 9-19
Luk 21: 12-15,24
Luk 23: 26-49
Luk 24: 45-48
Joh 1: 1-18,29
Joh 2: 13-17
Joh 3: 12-21,31-36
Joh 4: 1-54
Joh 5: 19-31
Joh 6: 35-40,44-58
Joh 7: 36
Joh 8: 12,25
Joh 9: 5
Joh 10: 1-18
Joh 11: 25-27,47,48
Joh 11: 51,52
Joh 12: 19
Joh 12: 20-33,37-40
Joh 13: 20,35
Joh 14: 15-31
Joh 15: 18-27
Joh 16: 5-11
Joh 17: 1-26
Joh 18: 33-37
Joh 19: 19-21
Joh 20: 21-23
Act 1: 1-10
Act 2: 1-41
Act 3: 11-26
Act 4: 16,23-25
Act 6: 1-7
Act 7: 1-8: 14
Act 8: 25-9: 16
Act 10: 1-11: 30
Act 13: 1-4,6-12,16
Act 13: 26,40-52

Act 14: 1,15-17
Act 14: 26-15: 35
Act 16: 1-10,16-40
Act 17: 4,10-12
Act 17: 16-34
Act 18: 6-8
Act 19: 17-20
Act 20: 21
Act 21: 19
Act 22: 21
Act 26: 1-30
Act 27: 1,2
Act 27: 21-28: 10
Act 28: 23-31
Rom 1: 1-6,8
Rom 1: 13-16,18-32
Rom 2: 1-29
Rom 3: 6,9-31
Rom 4: 9-25
Rom 5: 6-21
Rom 8: 18-23
Rom 9: 1-33
Rom 10: 4,11-20
Rom 11: 1-36
Rom 15: 7-33
Rom 16: 25
1Co 1: 18-25
1Co 3: 5-9
1Co 3: 21-4: 17
1Co 6: 9-11
1Co 7: 17-24
1Co 8: 5,6
1Co 9: 16-27
1Co 10: 31,32
1Co 12: 4-6,12,13
1Co 15: 20-28
2Co 2: 12-3: 3
2Co 4: 3,4,6
2Co 5: 14-21
2Co 10: 13-16
Gal 1: 4,5,15-17
Gal 2: 1-17
Gal 3: 8,9,14,16
Gal 3: 21-29
Gal 6: 14
Eph 1: 3-23

Eph 2: 11-3: 12
Eph 4: 4-6,20-24
Eph 6: 19,20
Php 1: 2-11
Php 2: 6-11
Col 1: 6,16-20,23-29
Col 2: 9-15
Col 3: 2-6
1Th 1: 2-10
1Th 2: 15-20
1Th 5: 1-11
2Th 1: 3-12
2Th 2: 11,12
1Ti 2: 1-8
1Ti 3: 16
1Ti 4: 9,10
2Ti 4: 1-4,17
Tit 2: 11-14
Heb 1: 1-3;6
Heb 5: 8-10
Heb 6: 13-19
Heb 7: 23-27
Heb 8: 1-2,6
Heb 9: 11-15,23-28
Heb 11: 8-19
Jam 1: 1
1Pe 1: 1,2
1Pe 2: 9-12
1Pe 3: 18-22
2Pe 3: 5-12
1Jo 3: 08
1Jo 4: 9-14
Rev 1: 4-8
Rev 2: 26-27
Rev 3: 10
Rev 4: 1-7: 17
Rev 8: 6-10: 11
Rev 11: 15-19
Rev 13: 1-15: 8
Rev 17: 13-18
Rev 18: 1-3
Rev 19: 1-16

Appendix C

What Now?

59 Action Steps for You and Your Church

You've caught a vision of God's heart for the nations. And you want to get into action. You desperately want to do something after you've been exposed to what God is up to in His word and in His works.

We'll list some possible action steps. But first a word of caution. These action steps are not to be a "compartment" of your life which you "dabble in" every now and then.

Don't allow them to be seen as one-time events, which is easy to do. Rather, see them as tools to help you integrate a world vision into your everyday life. The two should be inseparable.

Build and Act on the Vision: A To-Do List
Individual Action Steps

Commit Yourself

1. Write a letter to a distant best friend telling of your commitment to the vision of God's great purpose on earth—the top line and the bottom line.

2. List your top-line blessings and pray/meditate on how you can consecrate each one as a bottom-line blessing. Your life is a big "reception": What do you have that you have not received? How can these blessings be channeled into God's unchangeable purpose?

- spiritual gifts
- ethnic heritage
- big—even "negative"—events that shaped you
- education
- family traditions

- physical skills, talents
- supportive friends

3. Sign the "Caleb Declaration" of commitment:

> *"Then Caleb silenced the people before Moses and said, 'We should go up and take possession of the land, for we can certainly do it'" (Numbers 13:30).*

> *By the grace of God and for His glory, I commit my entire life to obeying His commission of Matthew 28:18-20 wherever and however He leads me, giving priority to the peoples currently beyond the reach of the Gospel (Romans 15:20-21).*

> *As an expression of my commitment, I will attempt to fulfill the following:*

> *(A) I will go to another culture or stay in this one, depending on the Lord's leading.*

> *(B) I will share my vision with other Christians, recognizing that my local church or campus student group are the obvious places for me to begin.*

> *(C) As others grow in commitment to Christ's global cause, I will trust that three of them will sign the Caleb Declaration.*

> *(D) To help me follow through with my commitment, I will "report" to someone (perhaps my pastor) monthly on how I am building and acting on this vision to reach every nation.*

> *Signature _____ Date _____*

(Consider photocopying this declaration and posting it where you'll see it often.)

4. Explore your role as a "priest" (I Peter 2:9-10). What does a priest do? How can you literally or figuratively perform those services for the unreached peoples of the world? The consecration rites of the sons of Aaron lasted seven

days. What could you do daily for a week that would cement in your memory that you are one of a people of God's possession, a holy nation, a kingdom of priests?

5. List activities you can do away with to better commit your time to God's purpose.

6. Raise an "Ebenezer" (I Samuel 7:12). Build a monument (a pile of stones, plaque, or slab of wet concrete) to acknowledge your determination to align your life with God's unchangeable purpose; then annually spend a full day commemorating and renewing your commitment.

7. If there is a possibility of your going to the field, ask around for a mission mentor you can be accountable to. Ask locally first, then check with your denomination. Finally, a national tracking and advising system operated by Caleb Project (1605 Elizabeth St., Pasadena, CA 91104) will encourage you to progress in your commitment levels.

Share

8. Compile your list of top-line blessings (see under step 2, p. 169) and ask others for clues as to other blessings you're not realizing in your life. You'll then have to explain the "blessed to be a blessing" principle!

9. Find one or two friends who will meet with you for a regular (weekly? bi-weekly? monthly?) unreached peoples prayer session. As you develop as a small group:
   - Help each other clarify your motives in mission interest.
   - Hold each other accountable for Bible study, prayer, and giving.
   - Encourage each other with global breakthroughs.

10. Set up a monthly global awareness book table in your church narthex. Set out pamphlets from your church's mission organizations, video and audio tapes, and study books to encourage others to catch the vision. Compile your own materials or contact William Carey Library (1705 N. Sierra Bonita Ave., Pasadena, CA 91104) for in-

formation on a pre-packaged library of materials called a World Christian Display Table.

Pray

11. Set up a "Nation's Prayer Reminder" system, perhaps as simple as a card with one unreached people group listed, to remind you to pray while you are doing dishes, taking a shower, jogging, etc.

12. Put a sticky label dot on your watch, your clock at home or work, and/or your car's rear view mirror to remind you to pray for the Lord of the harvest to thrust forth laborers.

13. Adopt a specific team overseas to pray for in the Muslim, Buddhist, Hindu, Tribal, or Chinese world. Contact Frontiers for information on a specific Muslim team.

14. Subscribe to the *Global Prayer Digest*. This monthly prayer guide features an unreached people group each day. You can join with thousands of other prayer warriors focusing on that group that day. Send for a sample or subscribe for $6 from *Global Prayer Digest* Subscriptions, 1605 Elizabeth St., Pasadena, CA 91104.

15. Get the book *Operation World: A Day-to-day Guide to Praying for the World* by Patrick Johnstone, to further guide your prayers for the unreached peoples of the earth. Order from your local Christian bookstore or through Frontiers, 325 N. Stapley Dr., Mesa, AZ 85203, 602/834-1500.

16. Beginning with those profiled in this book, pray over a list of unreached peoples. Once a month pray for them all at once, finding their locations on a world map. Perhaps "tithe" a Sunday and spend one-tenth of your day in prayer for the nations.

17. Attend a "Concert of Prayer" with your family or a group of friends. These prayer gatherings concentrate on revival, leading to "fullness"—God's blessing on us, His people—and "fulfillment"—His blessing on every people. For loca-

tions near you, contact: Concerts of Prayer International, P.O. Box 36008, Minneapolis, MN 55435.

Study

18. Review your understanding of the vision of "A Church for Every People by the Year 2000." Begin to memorize some of the passages cited in this study.

19. Evaluate the highlighted passages in your personal study Bible. How many of the passages refer to God's blessing the nations (bottom line) and how many refer to God's blessing you (top line)?

20. Buy a new Bible and underline the passages specifically referring to the bottom line—God's blessing for the nations.

21. Take the "Perspectives on the World Christian Movement" course which extensively covers the biblical, historical, cultural, and strategic aspects of God's plan to reach every people, tribe, tongue, and nation. Extension classes are offered throughout the world, and the course can be taken by correspondence. Contact the Perspectives Study Program, 1605 Elizabeth St., Pasadena, CA 91104.

22. Subscribe to a dozen or more mission magazines and newsletters. Some of the generic "must-reads" include:

• *Mission Frontiers,* Records Office, 1605 Elizabeth St., Pasadena, CA 91104.

• *Evangelical Missions Quarterly,* Box 794, Wheaton, IL 60189.

• *Pulse,* Box 794, Wheaton, IL 60189.

23. Read your Sunday newspaper and a national or large metropolitan Sunday newspaper and notice:

• The hot spots of the news around the world. How could God be using this incident to further His unchangeable plan to bless the nations?

• Any mention of unreached people groups. What is God

doing among them, even through problems and the wrath of men, to accomplish His great purpose? Determine how much time you'll devote weekly to thinking through world news relating to unreached people groups.

24. Study what is happening in North American business activity abroad. Be aware of what North America is exporting; think through how that is affecting the nations and pray accordingly.

25. Study the book *Serve As A Sender,* a surprising, step-by-step approach to being a fully equipped sender to your missionaries. Order from Emmaus Road International, 7150 Tanner Court, San Diego, CA 92111, 619/292-7020.

26. Compile a cassette library of missiological tapes that focus on the biblical, historical, cultural, and strategic factors of finishing the task of the Great Commission. As if you're on a self-study course and are cramming for a final exam, listen to these tapes while driving, jogging, or doing house or yard work. Such tapes are available from William Carey Library, Box 40129, Pasadena, CA 91114. Ask for a resource catalog listing audio and video titles.

27. Read and jot findings in books that focus on unreached peoples and finishing the task. An excellent basic library of these types of books is called The World Christian Bookshelf, with twelve basic books to study. Write or phone William Carey Library (1705 N. Sierra Bonita Ave., Pasadena, CA 91104, 818/798-0819).

28. Go to school. For information on schools offering various mission training programs, send for a copy of this year's *Great Commission Handbook* (Berry Publishing Services, 701 Main St., Evanston, IL 60202; 708/869-1573) or the *Evangelical Missions Quarterly Guide to Continuing Education* (Box 794, Wheaton IL 60189).

Align Your Lifestyle

29. Evaluate the Christian records and books you own. How

many of them are about God blessing you in top-line blessings? How many incorporate bottom-line topics? Work toward a balance in the input you and your family get from the music and literature in your home.

30. Shop carefully for any item. Find the lowest price and give away what you saved!

31. Collect your loose change daily, count it monthly, and deposit it. Then send a check for that amount to an unreached peoples project championed by your mission agency.

32. Find out the average salary of a minister in your denomination. If it is lower than your salary, adjust to it over a period of months or years. Perhaps cut $100 out of your budget each month or every two months until your level of living matches that average ministerial salary. Give what you save to your selected unreached peoples mission effort!

33. Consult a financial planner, and get help setting a specific plan to decrease debt and increase your giving to the frontier mission efforts of your church or mission agency.

Give Time

34. Write to missionaries working on the front lines. Get personal in your news of the home front. Send Sunday funny papers. Encourage. Don't expect an answer. Be cautious in writing any missionary working in restricted-access countries (check with your mission agency for guidelines).

35. Connect with a mission agency wanting to learn more about a particular unreached group and clip newspaper and magazine references about that people and its geographical area.

36. Volunteer five hours weekly to your church or mission agency in some effort to reach unreached peoples, regardless of how indirectly.

37. Visit your nearest Christian radio station and encourage them to air mission programs about unreached people groups. Some generic mission programs which don't request funds include "Around the World" with NewService 2000; "World Prayer 2000" with Jack McAllister, and Global Prayer Digest Radio Spots sponsored by Far East Broadcasting Corporation's Mission Vision Network, Box 1, La Mirada, CA 90637.

38. Volunteer to help in a local or regional international student ministry. Shock foreign students by being interested in not only what political country they are from, but what people they are from. If you find students who are from people groups who have no strong Christian witness, relay this information to the international student organization headquarters, your mission agency, and the Adopt-A-People Clearinghouse (1539 E. Howard St., Pasadena, CA 90114).

    You just may be hosting an international student who could be the first one of his or her people to come to Christ. Mission groups targeting that people group will be more than interested to follow up on that individual, as he or she could be helpful to teach language nuances, customs, and other valuable "inside" information. And, perhaps that one student will be the key, the evangelist who will plant a church and foster a movement to Christ in his or her own people group!

39. Find out if there are internationals from unreached people groups working or living in your community. Remember that individuals from most Muslim, Hindu, and Buddhist people will be from unreached groups. Start up relationships with these internationals, realizing again that they may be precisely the one family God has ordained to carry the Gospel back to their homeland! Contact Doorstep Opportunities (1605 Elizabeth St., Pasadena, CA 91104) for ideas on how to best minister cross-culturally in your area.

40. Use your vacation time here or overseas to help research an unreached people group or assist in pre-evangelism (relief work, literature distribution, etc.) in a major city with unreached people communities. Contact your unreached peoples focused mission agency for opportunities. Get a clear idea of short-term opportunities in *Stepping Out: A Guide to Short-Term Missions* available through YWAM Publishing, P.O. Box 55787, Seattle, WA 98155, 800/922-2143 or 206/771-1153.

41. Help with research. Link up with your mission agency or a group such as the "Adopt-A-People Clearinghouse" (1539 E. Howard St., Pasadena, CA 91104) and find out what needs to be found out about a particular people group. You'll be amazed at how much strategic research needed by the mission community has already been done in decades' worth of sociological and anthropological studies, just sitting in your nearest university library!

42. Draw a time line of your life from birth to death. Consider tithing a tenth of your "expected" life span to be involved full-time in sending or giving.

43. Contact a mission agency targeting unreached peoples and start corresponding about possible short-term and career assignments.

44. Research the possibilities of becoming a part-time or full-time mission mobilizer in your area. Learn how to share the vision with groups. Encourage prayer, giving and activism on behalf of the unreached. Contact your mission agency for ideas. Or, to become a generic mission mobilizer representing all evangelical mission groups, write Regional Office Coordinator of the U.S. Center for World Mission for information on serving in your area. Also, the Mobilization Division of the U.S. Center for World Mission can equip you with materials to encourage churches to "adopt" an unreached people group. Ask for

an Adopt-A-People Advocate Kit from U.S. Center for World Mission, 1605 Elizabeth St., Pasadena, CA 91104.

Action Steps for Your Fellowship Group or Church

Work with others, particularly the leadership of your church or fellowship group, to initiate the following educational steps in your group. Each of these resources is available through the U.S. Center for World Mission or a cooperating mission organization. (For information on resources, contact the Mobilization Division, U.S. Center for World Mission, 1605 Elizabeth St., Pasadena, CA 91104.)

45. Post Unreached Peoples Posters around your facility. These striking posters map out the details of the remaining task of reaching every people group for Christ.

46. Set out "Catch the Vision" brochures. These comprehensive pamphlets overview the biblical and strategic vision of finishing the task of the Great Commission. (Available in 10-packs through the U.S. Center for World Mission.)

47. Host a "Vision for the Nations" Sunday. This is a one-Sunday mission emphasis on the challenge of planting a church among each of the remaining unreached people groups. The packet includes Sunday school lessons for all ages, sermon outlines and samples, bulletin inserts for note-taking and responses, a small group Bible study guide on unreached peoples, and take-home prayer guides for the family. A stunning one-day mission emphasis!

48. Use the "Catch the Vision 2000" study course in adult Sunday School, in home-group Bible studies, at midweek services, or in Sunday evening sessions. The complete 12-session curriculum manual is available through William Carey Library, Box 40129, Pasadena, CA 91114.

49. For an even more intensive study of God's unchangeable purpose to bless every people with His offer of salvation, study through the video-based course of this study available through: Frontiers, 325 N. Stapley Dr., Mesa, AZ 85203, 1-800-GO2-THEM.

50. Since, as a group, you're getting out of the pew and into the battlefield, study through the nine-session video course on spiritual warfare available through Emmaus Road International, 7150 Tanner Court, San Diego, CA 92111, 619/292-7020.

51. Initiate a monthly mission fellowship in your church to study the implications of the biblical, historical, cultural, and strategic aspects of God's global purpose. The "Year of Vision" is a perfect program that provides video-based teaching guides for group discussion, instructions on how to pray daily for unreached peoples, and a plan for actually "adopting" an unreached people group. These twelve 90-minute sessions form an entire year's worth of mission education!

52. As a church, study your church's mission efforts:

- How can you better pray for and equip your missionaries to reached peoples to encourage nationals to become sending churches, sending their own missionaries to unreached peoples?
- How can you better pray for and equip your missionaries working among unreached groups?
- List all your missionaries and their locations on a sheet of paper and memorize them.

53. Begin to amplify and expand on your fellowship's mission educational foundation by hosting incisive seminars on various aspects of reaching the unreached. Some basic seminars ideal for inviting others to catch the foundational vision of God's global plan-include:

- Catch the Vision 2000 Seminar
- Destination 2000 Seminar
- A Mini-Perspectives Seminar

Other more specific aspects of what God is doing today are presented in specialized seminars including:

- Muslim Awareness Seminars

- China Awareness Seminars
- An Introduction to Cross-Cultural Ministry Seminars
- "Nothing Good Just Happens": 3-Day Cross-Cultural Ministry Training for Church Leadership.
  For information on booking any of the above seminars, contact the U.S. Center for World Mission Mobilization Division (1605 Elizabeth St., Pasadena, CA 91104) who will put you in touch with the organizations offering each.

54. Initiate the strategies and planning you will find in special handbooks from ACMC, Box 24762, Denver, CO 80224. Some of these include "Your Church Missions Policy Handbook," "Cultivating a Missions-Active Church," and "Missions Conference Planner." For ongoing help in mobilizing your church, consider joining ACMC or the Association of International Mission Services organization for charismatic-oriented congregations (AIMS, Box 64534, Virginia Beach, VA 23464).

55. Take specific steps to link with a mission agency targeting a specific people group; "adopt" a people! The varying degrees of responsibility your church can assume in this demanding enterprise are determined by you as a church and the agency. Contact your unreached-people-targeting mission agency or the Adopt-A-People Clearinghouse (1539 E. Howard St., Pasadena, CA 91104) for ideas on how to adopt an unreached group.

56. Send your pastor(s) to the field. Nothing will better infuse church leadership with a vision to help complete the Great Commission than a firsthand experience in researching or engaging an unreached group.

57. Send your pastor or other church leader to a mission agency, perhaps even to do clerical work! Nothing will help your church leadership sympathize more with the demands of mission work than seeing the support system operations at agency headquarters.

58. Send your pastor to the "Perspectives on the World Christian Movement" intensive course held each January on the campus of the U.S. Center for World Mission in Pasadena, California. Contact the Perspectives Study Course offices (1605 Elizabeth St., Pasadena, CA 91104) for details or for the location of the Perspectives extension course offered nearest you.

59. Hold a garage sale and give the money away to a mission agency working among a people not yet reached.

Enough Ideas to Prod Your Thinking?

Your own response to the vision of God's orchestration of world events to proclaim His character to every people, tribe, tongue, and nation, might never appear on such an action-step list. But since to whom much is given, much is required, your sense of that vision demands your response. What will you do?

If nothing else, do the foundational action step. Since you've had a chance to "look to the fields," get good at the basic response Jesus commanded: "Ask the Lord of the harvest, therefore, to send out workers into his harvestfield" (Matthew 9:38). Pray!

Prepared by Bill Stearns of the
U.S. Center for World Mission.

Appendix D
Compared Characteristics of Two Extreme Churches

A > B	A = B
Missions is seen as a one-week event.	World evangelization is in all aspects of the church throughout the year.
Only those who are "holy" or "called" get involved	Everyone has a role in evangelizing the world.
Missions is rarely mentioned in sermons outside missions week.	God's heart for the nations is heard in almost every sermon.
Adults decide on their own if God is "calling" them into missions.	Church leadership challenges couples and singles to consider going overseas.
It's "okay" if you want to go overseas short term.	Short terms are not only encouraged but developed within the church.
The terms *people groups* or *unreached peoples* are foreign to the average lay person.	Sunday school children are familiar with the terms *unreached peoples* or *people groups*.
The average attender can only name 2 - 3 verses that deal with missions.	The average lay person can name hundreds of verses, knowing God's heart for all nations is the theme of the Bible.
The idea of adopting a people group is foreign to them.	They are prayerfully considering or have already adopted a people group.
The first thing dropped in the church's budget is missions.	The pastor won't take a paycheck until all missionaries are paid.
Most members don't know who their missionaries are or where they're serving.	Most know who the church missionaries are, where they serve, and what their needs are.
Mission prayer meetings aren't usually held, and are poorly attended when held.	Mission prayer meetings are held consistently, well attended, and they join "Concerts of Prayer."
Few are even aware of the course "Perspectives on a World Christian Movement."	Many have taken "Perspectives" already and are encouraging others to do the same.
Missions and missionaries get as little money as possible.	The church is hoping to give 50% of their budget to missions.
Missions, though never stated, in reality is seen as a "necessary evil."	World evangelization is half the reason the church exists.

Appendix E

Creative Bottom-Line Verses to Familiar Children's Songs

THE B-I-B-L-E

The B-I-B-L-E
It has one story you see,
To reach all nations with God's love
the B-I-B-L-E

JESUS LOVES THE LITTLE CHILDREN

Jesus loves the unreached children,
All the unreached children of the world.
Muslims, Buddhists, Hin-dus,
Chinese, Tribals need Him, too.
Jesus died for all the children of the world.

IF YOU'RE BLESSED TO BE A BLESSING

If you're blessed to be a blessing, clap your hands (2X)
If you're blessed to be a blessing,
then your life will surely show it.
If you're blessed to be a blessing, clap your hands.

JESUS LOVES ME

Jesus loves the nations
Every tongue and every tribe
He wants to use you
To reach them to be His Bride.
Yes, Jesus loves them, (3X)
For the Bible tells me so.

OUR GOD IS AN AWESOME GOD

Our God is a faithful God
He keeps His promises
To reach all nations
Our God is a faithful God.

(Photocopy for further use.)

Appendix F

Order Form

T-Shirts   *(All prices include postage.)*

    Size: M _____ L _____ XL _____

    Qty. _____   X $12.85 = $ _____

    Picture: _____ Tennis Player or _____ Avant-Garde

Sweat Shirts:

    Size: M _____ L _____ XL _____

    Qty. _____   X $18.40 = $ _____

    Picture: _____ Tennis Player or _____ Avant-Garde

Books:

    Unveiled at Last! Qty. _____ X $9.50 = $ _____

    Becoming
    Unstoppable Qty. _____ X $9.50 = $ _____

Pictures:

    Qty. _____ Tennis _____ A-G   X $1.50 = $ _____

Destination 2000 in Video and Audio Series

Suggested Retail Price: Video: $139.95 Audio: $39.50
or "Whatever you can afford" (Write for more information.)

Rental of Video Series:

  # Months _____ X $25.00 per month = $ _____

Mail to: *(Please Print Clearly!)*

Name: _____

Address: _____

City _____ State _____ Zip: _____

Phone: _____

**Send to: Frontiers, 325 N. Stapley Dr., Mesa, AZ 85203,
602/834-1500.**

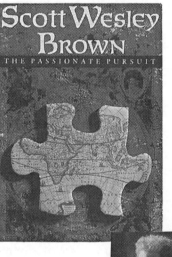